CONTENTS

BEYOND TEARS

Navigating The Journey Of Grief

Dr Bhaskar Bora

A PERSONAL NOTE FROM THE AUTHOR

My journey, once marked by certainty and driven by purpose, has transformed in ways I could never have anticipated. It is no longer about grand achievements or the pursuit of external success, but about the quiet, tender moments that reveal the true essence of life—moments of love, care, and presence. What you hold in your hands is not just a collection of words, but a testament to resilience, a story woven from the delicate threads of struggle, acceptance, and ultimately, renewal.

There was a time when my life flowed with the grace of a symphony, every note in perfect harmony. As a doctor, my days were filled with the pulse of life itself— offering hope, easing suffering, and healing with steady hands. The white coat I wore wasn't just a symbol of my profession; it embodied my very identity; an outward reflection of the healer I believed I was destined to be. The lives I touched, the people I helped—it all gave profound meaning to my existence.

But life, in its mysterious and unpredictable ways, had other plans. In one swift, unforeseen moment, the world I knew unraveled. First came the spinal cord injury, stripping away the physical strength I had relied upon. Then, the shadow of cancer darkened the horizon, a stark reminder of life's fragility. The world of medicine, where I once found so much joy and purpose, suddenly slipped away, leaving a vast emptiness in its wake—a silence where once there had been meaning.

Gone were the bustling corridors of the hospital, replaced by the quiet solitude of my home. No longer a "Doctor," I found myself standing at the edge of an uncertain future, my hands—once so steady with the knowledge of healing—trembling with questions I wasn't ready to face. Without the title, without the work that had defined me for so long, who was I? What was left of me when everything I had known was no longer within reach?
In that silence, in the stillness of a life interrupted, I began to uncover something unexpected. The role of a disabled husband and father, once a distant concept, became my new reality—one that held unexpected grace.

What began as an effort to nurture my relationships, to find solace in this new world, slowly evolved into a profound inward journey.

I found healing in the spiritual—a rhythm of meditation, reading, and reflection that allowed me to rediscover the parts of myself I thought were lost. As I immersed myself in books, audiobooks, and hours of research, I began to understand that this new chapter of my life was not an ending, but a rebirth. The solitude of these years, the quiet hours of writing and reflection, gave birth to the very pages you hold in your hands now.

It is with deep gratitude that I share these words with you, knowing that they carry with them not just knowledge but a piece of my soul. I hope that these reflections and insights offer you a fresh perspective on life and perhaps some nourishment for your own journey.

That we cannot control what the universe throws at us but how we react to those curveballs define who we are and what we make of our lives.

PROLOGUE

In the quiet moments when the world stands still, grief finds its way into our hearts, leaving a trail of sorrow, confusion, and pain. It is a universal experience, yet it feels profoundly personal, and unique to each of us in its intensity and depth. The loss of a loved one shakes the very foundation of our existence, challenging our sense of normalcy and forcing us to navigate a path we never wished to tread.

"Beyond Tears: Navigating the Journey of Grief" is

a compassionate companion for those who find themselves on this unwelcome journey. This book is born out of a deep understanding of the complexities of grief, informed by both professional expertise and personal experience. It aims to provide solace, guidance, and practical strategies to help you find your way through the darkness of loss.

As you turn these pages, you will encounter a blend of insightful information, poignant personal stories, and valuable resources designed to support you at every stage of your grieving process. From understanding the different types and stages of grief to discovering healthy coping mechanisms, this book offers a comprehensive guide to help you navigate your emotions and find a renewed sense of purpose.

You will read about individuals who have faced unimaginable losses and yet have found ways to heal and rebuild their lives. Their stories of resilience and hope serve as a testament to the indomitable human spirit and the possibility of finding light even in the darkest of times.

This book is not just for those who are grieving but also for those who support them. Friends, family members, and caregivers will find practical tips and insights to help them provide the empathy and understanding needed by those in mourning.

"Beyond Tears" is an invitation to embrace your grief, to acknowledge the pain, and to take small steps towards healing. It recognizes that the journey of grief is not linear and that there is no right or wrong way to grieve. Each person's path is unique, shaped by their experiences, relationships, and inner strength.

As you embark on this journey through the pages of this book, know that you are not alone. The stories and insights shared here are meant to offer you comfort and to remind you that it is possible to find hope and joy again, even after the profound loss of a loved one.

May "Beyond Tears" be a beacon of light in your darkest hours, guiding you towards healing, resilience, and a renewed sense of peace.

CHAPTER 1: UNDERSTANDING GRIEF

Introduction To Grief

Grief is a universal yet deeply personal experience that transcends cultural, social, and emotional boundaries. It is an intrinsic part of the human condition, reflecting the profound impact of loss on our lives. Whether it stems from the death of a loved one, the end of a significant relationship, or the loss of a cherished dream, grief shapes and reshapes our emotional landscape. To understand grief, we must delve into its complexities, acknowledging its universal aspects and the unique ways it manifests in each individual.

Grief is not merely a series of emotional responses but a multifaceted process encompassing a range of feelings, thoughts, and behaviours. It can bring about an overwhelming sense of sadness, despair, and longing, but it can also lead to feelings of anger, guilt, and confusion. These emotions often come in waves, ebbing and flowing unpredictably, and they can affect every aspect of a person's life.

The process of grieving is often compared to a journey, one that each person navigates in their own way and at their own pace. There is no right or wrong way to grieve, and there is no set timeline for how long the process should take. Some people may find solace and begin to heal relatively quickly, while others may struggle with their grief for many years. This journey is influenced by a variety of factors, including the nature of the loss, the individual's personality and coping mechanisms, their support system, and their cultural and religious beliefs.

Understanding grief requires recognizing that it is not a linear process. The notion that grief progresses through a series of predictable stages, leading to a final state of acceptance, is a simplification that does not capture the true nature of the experience. Instead, grief is often a cyclical process, with individuals revisiting different stages and emotions at various times. This cyclical nature means that even after a person seems to have moved forward, certain triggers or reminders can bring the grief back with renewed intensity.

One of the most challenging aspects of grief is its unpredictability. The feelings associated with grief can be triggered by seemingly innocuous events, such as a song on the radio, a familiar scent, or a specific date on the calendar. These triggers can evoke powerful memories and emotions, making it difficult for the grieving person to maintain a sense of stability. It is important for those who are grieving to recognize that these experiences are normal and that it is okay to feel overwhelmed at times.

Grief has a profound impact on a person's sense of identity and purpose. The loss of a loved one, in particular, can create a void that is difficult to fill. People may struggle with questions about their own existence and their place in the world without the presence of the person they have lost. This existential crisis can lead to a period of deep introspection and soul-searching, as individuals seek to find meaning and purpose in the aftermath of their loss.

The way people experience and express their grief is influenced by cultural and societal norms. Different cultures have their own rituals and traditions for mourning, and these practices can provide a framework for individuals to process their grief. In some cultures, public displays of mourning are encouraged, while in others, grief is considered a private matter to be dealt with quietly. Understanding these cultural differences is important for providing appropriate support to those who are grieving.

In addition to cultural influences, personal beliefs and values play a significant role in how individuals cope with grief. Religious and spiritual beliefs, in particular, can provide comfort and guidance during the grieving process. Many people find solace in the idea that their loved one is in a better place or that they will be reunited in the afterlife. Others may find comfort in nature, art, or other forms of personal expression.

While grief is an inevitable part of life, it is also a testament to the depth of our connections and the importance of our relationships. The pain of loss reflects the love and attachment we feel for those we have lost. In this sense, grief is a natural and necessary process that allows us to honour and remember our loved ones while also moving forward with our lives.

Understanding grief is the first step in navigating this challenging journey. By acknowledging the complexities and variations of grief, we can better support ourselves and others as we cope with loss. In the following chapters, we will explore the different types and stages of grief, the impact it has on our lives, and the ways we can cope and eventually find healing and hope.

Defining Grief and its Importance

Grief is often described as the deep sorrow and intense emotional suffering that follows a significant loss. While it is most commonly associated with the death of a loved one, grief can also arise from other forms of loss, such as the end of a relationship, the loss of a job, or the death of a pet. At its core, grief is the emotional response to the absence of someone or something that held a great significance in our lives.

The importance of grief lies in its role as a natural and necessary process for healing. It allows us to process our emotions, come to terms with our loss, and ultimately, find a way to move forward. Without the ability to grieve, we would be unable to fully experience and honour the depth of our connections and the impact of our losses.

Grief can manifest in a variety of ways, affecting our emotions, thoughts, behaviours, and physical health. Emotionally, grief often involves feelings of sadness, anger, guilt, and loneliness. These emotions can be intense and overwhelming, making it difficult to function in daily life. It is not uncommon for people to experience mood swings, crying spells, and a sense of hopelessness during the grieving process.

On a cognitive level, grief can lead to intrusive thoughts and memories of the loss. People may find themselves preoccupied with thoughts of their loved ones, replaying moments from their past, and imagining what their future could have been. This rumination can interfere with concentration, decision-making, and other cognitive functions, leading to a sense of mental fog or confusion.

Behaviourally, grief can impact our daily routines and activities. Some people may withdraw from social interactions, preferring to isolate themselves as they process their emotions. Others may engage in behaviours that are uncharacteristic, such as increased substance use, overeating, or other forms of self-medication. These behaviours are often coping mechanisms, attempts to numb the pain or find temporary relief from the intensity of grief.

Physically, grief can take a toll on the body. Common physical symptoms include fatigue, changes in appetite and sleep patterns, headaches, and a weakened immune system. The stress of grief can also exacerbate existing health conditions, making it important for individuals to pay attention to their physical well-being during this time.

Understanding the multifaceted nature of grief helps us recognize that it is a normal and healthy response to loss. It is not something that needs to be "fixed" or "cured," but rather, something that needs to be experienced and processed. Each person's grief journey is unique, and there is no right or wrong way to grieve. What matters most is finding ways to cope and support oneself through the process.

Grief also serves as a reminder of the deep connections we share with others. The pain of loss reflects the love and attachment we feel, and it is through grieving that we honour these bonds. In this sense, grief is a testament to the significance of our relationships and the impact they have on our lives.

As we navigate the grieving process, it is important to acknowledge and validate our emotions. Grieving can be a lonely and isolating experience but knowing that our feelings are normal and that others have experienced similar pain can provide a sense of comfort and solidarity. Sharing our grief with trusted friends, family members, or support groups can also help us feel less alone and more understood.

Grief is a powerful force that can transform us in profound ways. While it is often associated with pain and suffering, it also has the potential to lead to growth and healing. Through grief, we can gain a deeper understanding of ourselves, our relationships, and our capacity for resilience. It can inspire us to cherish the present moment, appreciate the people in our lives, and find new meaning and purpose.

In the chapters that follow, we will explore the various aspects of grief in greater detail, including the different types of grief, the stages of the grieving process, and the impact it has on our lives. By gaining a deeper understanding of grief, we can better navigate our own journeys and support others who are grieving.

Types of Grief

Grief is a complex and multifaceted experience that can take on many different forms. Understanding the various types of grief can help us recognize and validate our own experiences, as well as those of others. While grief is unique to each individual, several common types are widely recognized by mental health professionals.

1. Normal Grief:
Normal grief, also known as uncomplicated grief, is the most common form of grief. It encompasses the range of emotional, cognitive, and physical reactions that people typically experience after a loss. These reactions may include sadness, anger, confusion, and physical symptoms such as fatigue and changes in appetite. Normal grief usually follows a trajectory where the intensity of these reactions gradually decreases over

time, allowing the person to adjust to their loss and find a new sense of normalcy.

2. Anticipatory Grief:

Anticipatory grief occurs when a loss is expected but has not yet happened. This type of grief is often experienced by individuals who are facing the impending death of a loved one due to a terminal illness. Anticipatory grief allows people to begin the process of mourning before the actual loss occurs, giving them time to prepare emotionally and practically. While it can provide an opportunity for closure and meaningful goodbyes, it can also bring about feelings of anxiety and prolonged stress.

3. Complicated Grief:

Complicated grief, also known as prolonged grief disorder, occurs when the grieving process is prolonged and intensified, interfering with a person's ability to function in daily life. Individuals experiencing complicated grief may find themselves stuck in a state of chronic mourning, with persistent and intrusive thoughts about the deceased, intense yearning, and difficulty accepting the loss. This type of grief often requires professional intervention to help the person process their emotions and move forward.

4. Disenfranchised Grief:

Disenfranchised grief refers to grief that is not acknowledged or validated by society. This can occur when the loss is considered insignificant or when the relationship between the griever and the deceased is not recognized. Examples include the loss of a pet, the death of an ex-partner, or the loss of a same-sex partner in a society that does not accept the relationship. Disenfranchised grief can lead to feelings of isolation and a lack of support, making it difficult for the individual to process their emotions.

5. Ambiguous Loss:

Ambiguous loss is a type of grief that occurs when there is uncertainty about the nature of the loss. This can happen when a loved one is physically absent but psychologically present, such as in cases of missing persons or dementia. Ambiguous loss creates a sense of unresolved grief, as there is no clear closure or understanding of the situation. It can lead to feelings of confusion, helplessness, and prolonged distress.

6. Cumulative Grief:

Cumulative grief occurs when an individual experiences multiple losses within a short period of time. The compounded effect of these losses can overwhelm the person's coping abilities, making it difficult to process each loss individually. Cumulative grief can lead to heightened emotional reactions, increased stress, and a greater risk of complicated grief.

7. Secondary Losses:

Secondary losses are the additional losses that occur as a result of the primary loss. Imagine the death of a spouse may lead to secondary losses such as financial instability, changes in social status, and the loss of shared dreams and future plans. These secondary losses can compound the grieving process, adding layers of complexity to the individual's emotional experience.

Understanding the different types of grief helps us recognize the diverse ways in which people experience and express their sorrow. It also underscores the importance of providing tailored support and validation for each individual's unique grieving process. By acknowledging the various forms of grief, we can foster a more compassionate and inclusive approach to supporting those who are mourning.

The Role of Culture in Grieving

Culture plays a significant role in shaping how individuals experience and express their grief. Cultural norms, traditions, and rituals influence how people mourn, providing a framework for understanding and processing their emotions. These cultural practices can offer comfort and support, but they can also create challenges for those whose grieving process does not align with societal expectations.

In many cultures, grief is expressed through specific rituals and ceremonies that honour the deceased and provide a sense of closure for the living. These rituals can include funerals, memorial services, and various mourning practices, such as wearing specific clothing, observing periods of silence, or participating in communal gatherings. These traditions offer a structured way for individuals to express their sorrow and receive support from their community.

Imagine in some African cultures, mourning rituals involve communal activities such as singing, dancing, and storytelling. These practices help to celebrate the life of the deceased and reinforce social bonds among the mourners. In contrast, many Western cultures emphasize more subdued and private expressions of grief, with an emphasis on individual mourning and personal reflection.

Religious beliefs also play a crucial role in shaping how people grieve. Many religions offer specific rituals and practices that provide comfort and a sense of continuity in the face of loss. Think about in Christianity, the concept of an afterlife and the promise of resurrection can offer solace to the bereaved. In Hinduism, the belief in reincarnation and the cycle of life and death can provide a framework for understanding and accepting loss.

However, cultural expectations around grief can sometimes create challenges for individuals whose experiences do not align with these norms. Imagine in cultures where stoicism and emotional restraint are valued, individuals may feel pressured to suppress their grief, leading to feelings of isolation and unprocessed emotions. Conversely, in cultures that emphasize expressive mourning, those who naturally grieve more privately may feel misunderstood or judged.

It is important to recognize that cultural practices and beliefs around grief are not monolithic; they can vary widely within a single culture based on factors such as age, gender, socioeconomic status, and personal experiences. Think about younger generations may adopt different grieving practices than their elders, influenced by globalization and changing social norms.

In multicultural societies, individuals may navigate multiple cultural influences in their grieving process. This can create a unique set of challenges and opportunities, as people blend traditional practices with new rituals that resonate with their personal experiences. Imagine a person from a multicultural background might incorporate elements from their family's cultural heritage along with contemporary practices that they find meaningful.

Understanding the role of culture in grieving allows us to provide more empathetic and culturally sensitive support to those who are mourning. It highlights the importance of respecting diverse grieving practices and recognizing that there is no one "right" way to grieve. By honouring each person's cultural background and individual preferences, we can create a more inclusive and compassionate environment for healing.

Personal Story - Marie's Journey

Marie sat quietly in her favourite armchair, clutching a faded photograph of her late husband, Antoine. It had been three years since his passing, but the pain still felt fresh, like an open wound that refused to heal. They had shared forty beautiful years together, raising three children and building a life filled with love and laughter. Antoine's sudden heart attack had shattered Marie's world, leaving her adrift in a sea of sorrow.

In the beginning, Marie's grief was all-consuming. She struggled to get out of bed, her days blurring into a haze of tears and numbness. Friends and family tried to offer their support, but their words often felt hollow and inadequate. "He's in a better place," they would say, or "Time heals all wounds." But Marie knew that time alone was not enough to mend her broken heart.

Marie found some solace in the rituals of her Catholic faith. The weekly Mass, the prayers, and the lighting of candles provided a sense of structure and connection to something greater than herself. Yet, even in the comforting embrace of her church community, there were moments when she felt utterly alone in her grief.

It was during one of these difficult days that Marie discovered a local support group for widows and widowers. Reluctantly, she decided to attend a meeting, unsure of what to expect. As she entered the room, she was greeted by warm smiles and empathetic nods. For the first time since Antoine's death, Marie felt a glimmer of hope.

The group met every Thursday evening, and over time, Marie began to form deep connections with the other members. They shared their stories, their struggles, and their small victories. In this circle of trust, Marie found the understanding and validation she had been yearning for. She realized that her grief was not a burden to be borne alone, but a shared human experience that connected her to others.

One evening, as Marie recounted a cherished memory of Antoine, she noticed that her tears were no longer only of sadness but also of joy. She was grateful for the love they had shared and the life they had built together. This realization marked a turning point in Marie's grieving journey. She began to see that her grief was not just a reflection of her loss, but also a testament to the depth of her love.

With the support of her new friends and the strength of her faith, Marie gradually started to rebuild her life. She volunteered at her church, started a small garden in Antoine's memory, and reconnected with her children and grandchildren. Though the pain of loss remained, it was no longer the defining feature of her existence.

Instead, it had become a part of her story, a chapter in a life that continued to unfold.

Marie's journey through grief taught her that healing is not about forgetting or moving on, but about finding a way to carry the memory of our loved ones with us as we move forward. It is about honouring the past while embracing the present and the future. And most importantly, it is about allowing us to feel, to mourn, and to eventually find hope and joy once again.

CHAPTER 2: THE STAGES OF GRIEF

Introduction To The Stages Of Grief

Grief is often a turbulent and unpredictable journey, marked by a wide range of emotions and experiences. To help make sense of this process, many mental health professionals refer to the concept of stages of grief. These stages, first introduced by psychiatrist Elisabeth Kübler-Ross in her groundbreaking work on death and dying, provide a framework for understanding the common emotional responses to loss. While not everyone will experience all of these stages or in the same order, they offer a valuable lens through which to view the grieving process.

The five stages of grief, as outlined by Kübler-Ross, include denial, anger, bargaining, depression, and acceptance. Each stage represents a different aspect of the emotional and psychological journey that individuals may go through as they cope with loss. It is important to remember that these stages are not linear; people may move back and forth between stages, experience several stages simultaneously, or skip stages altogether. Grief is a deeply personal experience, and each person's journey is unique.

Denial is often the first stage of grief. It serves as a protective mechanism, allowing individuals to gradually absorb the reality of their loss. During this stage, people may struggle to accept that the loss has occurred, feeling numb or in shock. Denial helps to buffer the immediate impact of the loss, giving the mind time to process the overwhelming emotions that come with it.

As the reality of the loss begins to set in, anger may emerge. This stage is characterized by feelings of frustration, helplessness, and even rage. Individuals may direct their anger toward themselves, others, or the circumstances surrounding the loss. Anger can be a powerful and intense emotion, but it is a natural part of the grieving process. It allows individuals to express their pain and can provide a sense of control in an otherwise uncontrollable situation.

Bargaining often follows anger. During this stage, individuals may find themselves making deals or promises, hoping to reverse or lessen the impact of the loss. This can involve thoughts like, "If only I had done this differently," or "I promise to do better if I can have them back." Bargaining is an attempt to regain control and find meaning in the face of loss. It reflects the deep desire to change the outcome and avoid the pain of grief.

As the reality of the loss becomes more apparent, individuals may enter the stage of depression. This stage is marked by profound sadness, despair, and a sense of emptiness. Individuals may withdraw from social activities, lose interest in things they once enjoyed, and experience changes in appetite and sleep patterns. Depression can be one of the most challenging stages of grief, as it involves confronting the full weight of the loss and the void it has created.

The final stage, acceptance, involves coming to terms with the loss. Acceptance does not mean that the pain of grief is gone, but rather that individuals have found a way to integrate the loss into their lives. They begin to adjust to a new reality, finding ways to move forward while honouring the memory of their loved one. Acceptance is about finding peace and a sense of closure, allowing individuals to live a fulfilling life despite their loss.

While Kübler-Ross's model provides a helpful framework for understanding grief, it is important to recognize that not everyone will experience these stages in the same way. Grief is a highly individual process, influenced by a variety of factors including personality, cultural background, and the nature of the loss. Some people may find that they do not fit neatly into these stages, and that is perfectly normal. The key is to acknowledge and validate one's own unique journey through grief.

In the pages that follow, we will explore each of these stages in greater detail, examining the emotions, thoughts, and behaviours associated with each stage. By gaining a deeper understanding of the stages of grief, we can better navigate our own grieving process and offer more compassionate support to others who are mourning.

Denial

Denial is often the initial response to a significant loss,

acting as a protective barrier that shields us from the immediate impact of grief. When we experience a loss, our minds may struggle to comprehend the full extent of what has happened. Denial allows us to gradually process the reality of the situation, giving us time to absorb the emotional shock.

In the stage of denial, individuals may feel numb or disconnected from their emotions. They might find themselves thinking, "This can't be happening," or "It must be a mistake." This disbelief can manifest in various ways, from a refusal to acknowledge the loss to a sense of detachment from the world around them. Imagine someone who has lost a loved one might continue to set a place at the dinner table for them or expect them to walk through the door at any moment.

Denial serves an important function by providing a temporary respite from the overwhelming emotions of grief. It allows individuals to continue functioning in their daily lives, even if they are not fully engaging with their emotions. This stage can be especially prominent in sudden or traumatic losses, where the mind needs more time to adjust to the new reality.

However, prolonged denial can hinder the grieving process and prevent individuals from moving forward. It is essential to gently confront and acknowledge the reality of the loss, even if it is painful. This can involve talking about the loss with trusted friends or family members, seeking professional counselling, or participating in rituals that honour the deceased.

Consider a person who lost their partner in a car accident might initially refuse to believe that their loved one is truly gone. They might continue to call their partner's phone or keep their belongings untouched. Over time, with support and encouragement, they may begin to accept the loss, allowing themselves to grieve and remember their partner in meaningful ways.

It is important to approach denial with compassion and patience, both for oneself and for others. Recognizing that denial is a natural part of the grieving process can help reduce feelings of guilt or shame. Instead of forcing oneself to "snap out of it," it is more helpful to gently encourage the acknowledgement of the loss while providing support and understanding.

Denial can also manifest in subtle ways, such as minimizing the significance of the loss or avoiding situations that remind us of it. Think about someone who has lost a job they loved might downplay the impact it has on their identity and future plans. They might avoid talking about it or pretend that they are unaffected. Acknowledging these forms of denial is crucial for addressing the underlying emotions and beginning the healing process.

As individuals move through the stage of denial, they may experience a gradual shift in their emotions. The numbness and disbelief may give way to more intense feelings of anger, sadness, or confusion. This transition can be challenging, but it is a necessary step in the grieving process. It allows individuals to begin processing their emotions and moving toward healing.

Supporting someone in the stage of denial involves offering a non-judgmental and empathetic presence. Encourage open conversations about the loss and validate their feelings, even if they seem contradictory or confusing. Remind them that it is okay to take their time and that their grief journey is unique to them.

Ultimately, moving through denial is about finding a balance between protecting oneself from overwhelming pain and allowing oneself to experience and process the emotions associated with loss. It is a delicate and personal journey, but one that is essential for healing and growth.

Anger

As the reality of loss begins to set in, many individuals find themselves grappling with feelings of anger. This stage of grief can be intense and disorienting, as the anger may be directed at various targets, including oneself, others, or even the deceased. Anger is a natural and valid response to loss, reflecting the deep sense of injustice and helplessness that often accompanies grief.

Anger can manifest in numerous ways, from irritability and frustration to outright rage. Individuals may feel angry at the circumstances of the loss, questioning why it happened and how it could have been prevented. They might direct their anger toward themselves, feeling guilty or blaming themselves for not doing more. Others may become angry at friends, family members, or medical professionals, feeling that they did not do enough to prevent the loss.

A woman who loses her father to a long battle with cancer might feel angry at the doctors for not finding a cure, angry at herself for not spending more time with him, and angry at her father for leaving her. These conflicting emotions can create a tumultuous inner experience, making it difficult to find peace.

Anger serves several important functions in the grieving process. It provides an outlet for the intense emotions that accompany loss, allowing individuals to express their pain and frustration. It can also be a way to assert control in a situation that feels overwhelmingly uncontrollable. By directing their anger outward, individuals may feel a temporary sense of empowerment and release.

However, prolonged or unaddressed anger can have detrimental effects on one's mental and physical health. It can lead to strained relationships, increased stress, and a prolonged sense of bitterness. Finding healthy ways to express and manage anger is crucial for navigating this stage of grief.

One effective approach is to channel anger into constructive activities. Physical exercise, creative expression, and community service can provide positive outlets for the intense energy that anger generates. Engaging in these activities can help individuals feel more grounded and balanced, reducing the impact of anger on their overall well-being.

Imagine a man who loses his brother in a tragic accident might take up running as a way to cope with his anger. The physical exertion provides a release for his pent-up emotions, and the routine of running offers a sense of stability and control. Over time, he may find that his anger lessens, replaced by a sense of accomplishment and resilience.

Talking about one's anger can also be a powerful tool for healing. Sharing feelings with a trusted friend, family member, or therapist can provide validation and support. It allows individuals to explore the underlying emotions driving their anger, such as fear, sadness, or guilt. By understanding these deeper feelings, individuals can begin to address them more directly, reducing the intensity of their anger.

Think about a young woman who feels angry after the death of her mother might benefit from speaking with a grief counsellor. Through these conversations, she may uncover feelings of abandonment and fear that are fuelling her anger. By addressing these root causes, she can begin to find ways to soothe her pain and move toward acceptance.

Practicing mindfulness and relaxation techniques can also help manage anger. Techniques such as deep breathing, meditation, and progressive muscle relaxation can reduce the physical and emotional intensity of anger. These practices promote a sense of calm and presence, helping individuals feel more in control of their emotions.

It is important to approach the stage of anger with compassion and patience. Recognize that anger is a natural part of the grieving process and that it is okay to feel these intense emotions. Instead of judging oneself or others for feeling angry, focus on finding healthy ways to express and process these feelings.

Supporting someone in the stage of anger involves providing a safe and non-judgmental space for them to express their emotions. Listen actively, validate their feelings, and offer practical support as needed. Encourage them to explore healthy outlets for their anger and remind them that it is okay to seek help if the anger feels overwhelming.

Ultimately, moving through the stage of anger is about finding balance and healing. It is a journey of acknowledging and honouring one's pain, while also seeking ways to transform and release it. By navigating this stage with awareness and support, individuals can move toward a place of greater peace and acceptance.

Bargaining

The stage of bargaining is often characterized by a deep yearning to change the reality of the loss. During this stage, individuals may find themselves engaging in "what if" and "if only" thinking, as they try to make sense of their loss and find a way to mitigate their pain. Bargaining is a natural response to the helplessness and vulnerability that accompany grief, reflecting a desire to regain control and find meaning.

In the bargaining stage, individuals may attempt to negotiate with a higher power, themselves, or the circumstances surrounding the loss. They might make promises or deals, hoping that by doing so, they can reverse or lessen the impact of the loss. Common thoughts during this stage include, "If only I had done this differently," "I promise to be a better person if I can have them back," or "What if I had noticed the signs sooner?"

Bargaining often involves a sense of guilt or

responsibility, as individuals reflect on their actions and decisions leading up to the loss. They may replay events in their minds, searching for ways they could have prevented the loss or done things differently. This self-examination can be painful, as it brings to light feelings of regret and self-blame.

Imagine a father who loses his teenage son in a car accident might find himself thinking, "If only I had insisted he stay home that night," or "I promise to be a better parent if I can have him back." These thoughts reflect a deep longing to change the past and alleviate the pain of loss.

While bargaining can provide a temporary sense of control, it is ultimately a way of grappling with the reality of the loss. It reflects the human tendency to seek meaning and purpose in the face of suffering. However, it is important to recognize that no amount of bargaining can change the past and that healing involves accepting the loss and finding ways to move forward.

One way to navigate the bargaining stage is to acknowledge and validate these thoughts and feelings without judgment. Understand that bargaining is a natural part of the grieving process and that it reflects the deep love and attachment one feels for the person or thing that was lost. Allow yourself to feel these emotions and to express them in healthy ways.

Talking about your thoughts and feelings with a trusted friend, family member, or therapist can provide support and perspective. Sharing your experiences can help you feel less isolated and more understood, and it can provide valuable insights into your grieving process. Imagine a woman who loses her best friend to a chronic illness might find comfort in talking to a grief counsellor. Through these conversations, she can explore her feelings of guilt and regret, and begin to find ways to cope with her loss.

Engaging in self-compassion and self-care is also crucial during this stage. Recognize that it is okay to feel vulnerable and that it is important to take care of yourself. This might involve setting aside time for rest and relaxation, engaging in activities that bring you joy, or seeking support from loved ones. By taking care of yourself, you can build resilience and strength to navigate the challenges of grief.

It can also be helpful to find ways to honour and remember the person or thing that was lost. Creating rituals or memorials, such as planting a tree, creating a scrapbook, or participating in a charity event, can provide a sense of meaning and connection. These acts of remembrance can help you feel closer to your loved one and provide a way to channel your grief into positive action.

Think about a mother who loses her daughter to a rare disease might start a foundation in her daughter's name to raise awareness and funds for research. This act of service can provide a sense of purpose and fulfilment, helping her to find meaning in her loss.

Supporting someone in the bargaining stage involves listening with empathy and understanding. Avoid dismissing their feelings or offering platitudes, and instead, provide a safe space for them to express their thoughts and emotions. Encourage them to seek support and remind them that it is okay to ask for help.

Ultimately, moving through the bargaining stage is about finding a balance between acknowledging the pain of the past and finding ways to move forward. It is a journey of self-discovery and healing, as individuals come to terms with their loss and seek new ways to live a meaningful and fulfilling life.

Depression

The depression stage of grief is often one of the most challenging and profound parts of the grieving process. This stage is marked by deep sadness, despair, and a sense of emptiness as individuals fully confront the reality of their loss. Unlike clinical depression, which is a mental health disorder, the depression experienced during grief is a natural and expected response to significant loss.

During the depression stage, individuals may feel overwhelmed by the weight of their emotions. They might experience persistent feelings of sadness, hopelessness, and a lack of interest or pleasure in activities they once enjoyed. Physical symptoms, such as changes in appetite and sleep patterns, fatigue, and difficulty concentrating, are also common. This stage can feel isolating and all-consuming, as the loss becomes an ever-present reality.

Depression in grief is a normal and necessary part of the healing process. It allows individuals to process the depth of their loss and to mourn the absence of their loved one or cherished thing. This stage often involves a period of introspection and reflection, as individuals grapple with the impact of their loss on their identity, relationships, and future.

Imagine a woman who loses her husband of fifty years might find herself struggling to get out of bed, feeling overwhelmed by the void his absence has created. She may withdraw from social activities, lose interest in hobbies they once shared, and feel a profound sense of loneliness. These experiences reflect the deep sorrow and adjustment that come with such a significant loss.

Navigating the depression stage requires patience, self-compassion, and support. It is important to allow yourself to feel and express your emotions, even if they are painful. Bottling up or suppressing these feelings can prolong the grieving process and prevent healing. Instead, find healthy ways to express your emotions, such as talking to a trusted friend, writing in a journal, or engaging in creative activities like painting or music.

Seeking professional support can also be beneficial during this stage. A grief counsellor or therapist can provide a safe and supportive space to explore your feelings and work through the challenges of grief. They can offer tools and strategies to help you cope with the intensity of your emotions and begin the process of healing.

Think about a man who lost his mother to Alzheimer's disease might find it helpful to join a support group for caregivers. Sharing his experiences with others who understand his pain can provide validation and comfort, and it can help him feel less alone in his grief. Through these connections, he can find strength and resilience to navigate the difficult emotions he is facing.

Engaging in self-care is crucial during the depression stage. This involves taking care of your physical, emotional, and mental well-being. Prioritize activities that nurture and soothe you, whether it is spending time in nature, practising mindfulness and relaxation techniques, or seeking comfort in spiritual or religious practices. These activities can provide a sense of grounding and stability, helping you to cope with the waves of sadness that may come and go.

It is also important to reach out for support from friends, family, or community members. While it can be tempting to isolate yourself, staying connected with others can provide a valuable source of comfort and encouragement. Letting others know what you need, whether it is a listening ear, practical help, or simply their presence, can make a significant difference in your grieving journey.

A young woman who loses her best friend might find solace in spending time with mutual friends who shared similar experiences. Together, they can reminisce about their friend, share their feelings, and support each other through the grieving process. These connections can provide a sense of continuity and remind her that she is not alone in her grief.

Supporting someone in the depression stage involves being present and offering a compassionate and non-judgmental space for them to express their emotions. Avoid trying to "fix" their pain or offering unsolicited advice. Instead, listen actively, validate their feelings, and offer practical support as needed. Encourage them to seek professional help if they are struggling to cope with their emotions.

Ultimately, moving through the depression stage is about finding a way to integrate the loss into your life. It is a journey of accepting the reality of the loss, mourning the absence, and finding ways to rebuild and move forward. This process takes time and patience, but with support and self-compassion, it is possible to find hope and healing.

Acceptance

Acceptance is often considered the final stage of the grieving process. It involves coming to terms with the reality of the loss and finding a way to move forward while honouring the memory of what was lost. Acceptance does not mean that the pain of grief is gone, but rather that individuals have found a way to integrate the loss into their lives and to live meaningfully despite it.

During the acceptance stage, individuals may begin to adjust to their new reality. They find ways to adapt to the changes brought about by the loss and to create a new sense of normalcy. This stage often involves a sense of peace and resolution, as individuals come to understand that the loss is a part of their story but does not define their entire existence.

Acceptance is a gradual process that can take time and effort. It is not about forgetting or moving on, but about finding a way to live with the loss and to carry the memory of the loved one or cherished thing in a healthy and meaningful way. This stage often involves a combination of emotional, cognitive, and behavioural adjustments as individuals learn to navigate their new reality.

Imagine a woman who loses her child might find ways to honour their memory by participating in activities that were important to them, such as volunteering for a charity they supported or creating a memorial garden in their name. These acts of remembrance provide a sense of connection and continuity, allowing her to carry her child's memory forward in a positive way.

Acceptance also involves finding new sources of meaning and purpose. This might include pursuing new interests, setting new goals, or building new relationships. By focusing on the present and the future, individuals can find a sense of fulfilment and joy despite their loss.

Think about a man who loses his wife to a long illness might decide to write a book about their life together, sharing their story with others and preserving her memory. This project can provide a sense of purpose and accomplishment, helping him to find a way to move forward while honouring their love.

It is important to recognize that acceptance does not mean that the pain of grief is completely gone. There will still be moments of sadness and longing, especially around anniversaries or significant dates. However, acceptance allows individuals to navigate these moments with greater resilience and to find ways to celebrate the life and memory of their loved one.

Supporting someone in the acceptance stage involves acknowledging their journey and providing encouragement as they find their way forward. Offer to participate in activities that honour their loved one's memory, celebrate their achievements, and remind them of their strength and resilience. Be present and supportive, recognizing that the journey of grief is ongoing and that acceptance is a dynamic and evolving process.

Ultimately, acceptance is about finding a way to live a meaningful and fulfilling life despite the loss. It is a testament to the strength of the human spirit and the capacity to heal and grow. By embracing acceptance, individuals can find a sense of peace and hope, allowing them to carry their loved one's memory forward in a positive and life-affirming way.

CHAPTER 3: PERSONAL STORIES OF LOSS & GRIEF

C.S. Lewis and "A Grief Observed"

C.S. Lewis, the renowned author of "The Chronicles of Narnia," faced profound grief after the death of his wife, Joy Davidman. His deeply personal and raw reflections on his grief journey are captured in his book "A Grief Observed." Lewis's story offers a poignant and relatable exploration of the complexities of grief and the process of finding meaning after loss.

C.S. Lewis met Joy Davidman, an American poet and writer, later in life. Their relationship began as a close friendship, marked by intellectual and spiritual connections. Joy's vivacious personality and sharp wit captivated Lewis, and their bond deepened over time. Despite their initial hesitations, they eventually married, finding profound joy and companionship in each other.

However, their happiness was short-lived. Joy was diagnosed with cancer, and despite initial signs of remission, her health deteriorated. Lewis devoted himself to her care, experiencing moments of hope and despair as they navigated the challenges of her illness. Joy's eventual death left Lewis devastated, grappling with a profound sense of loss and the disintegration of the life they had built together.

In the aftermath of Joy's death, Lewis channelled his grief into writing. "A Grief Observed" is a collection of his personal reflections and journal entries during this period. The book is a raw and unfiltered account of his emotional turmoil, capturing the depth of his sorrow, anger, and confusion. Lewis's honesty and vulnerability resonate with readers, offering a window into the deeply personal experience of grief.

One of the most striking aspects of "A Grief Observed" is Lewis's candid exploration of his faith. As a devout Christian, Lewis had often written about the nature of God and suffering. However, in the face of Joy's death, he found himself questioning his beliefs and struggling to reconcile his faith with his grief. He described feeling abandoned by God and grappling with the silence and seeming absence of divine comfort.

Lewis's reflections on faith and doubt are particularly poignant for those who wrestle with similar questions in their grief journey. His honesty about his spiritual struggles provides a sense of validation and understanding for those who may feel isolated in their doubts. Ultimately, Lewis's journey led him to a deeper and more nuanced understanding of his faith, marked by a recognition of the complexities of suffering and the mystery of the divine.

"A Grief Observed" also captures the raw and often contradictory emotions that accompany grief. Lewis writes about the oscillation between intense sorrow and moments of numbness, the longing for his wife and the struggle to accept her absence. His reflections on the physical and emotional impact of grief provide a relatable and empathetic portrayal of the grieving process.

Imagine Lewis describes the physical sensation of grief as a "sort of invisible blanket between the world and me." This vivid imagery captures the sense of disconnection and isolation that many people experience in their grief. His descriptions of the emotional landscape of grief —ranging from deep despair to fleeting moments of acceptance—resonate with readers who have navigated similar terrain.

Despite the depth of his sorrow, Lewis's journey through grief is also marked by moments of insight and growth. He reflects on the enduring impact of his relationship with Joy and the ways in which her memory continues to shape his life. His journey illustrates that while the pain of loss may never completely disappear, it is possible to find moments of meaning, connection, and even joy amidst the sorrow.

C.S. Lewis's story and his reflections in "A Grief Observed" offer a powerful testament to the complexities of grief and the resilience of the human spirit. His willingness to confront his emotions and question his beliefs provides a model of authenticity and courage for those navigating their own grief journeys. By sharing his experiences, Lewis offers a sense of companionship and understanding, reminding readers that they are not alone in their sorrow.

Michelle Obama and Her Father's Death

Michelle Obama, the former First Lady of the United States, faced a profound loss when her father, Fraser Robinson III, passed away from complications related to multiple sclerosis. Her reflections on this loss, as shared in her memoir "Becoming," offer insights into the impact of grief and the journey of healing.

Fraser Robinson III was a central figure in Michelle Obama's life. Known for his hardworking nature, integrity, and unwavering support for his family, Fraser instilled in Michelle the values of perseverance, resilience, and community. Despite his battle with multiple sclerosis, he remained a steadfast presence in his children's lives, inspiring them with his determination and love.

Michelle's father's death left a significant void in her life. She describes the profound impact of his loss on her emotional well-being and the challenge of navigating life without his guidance and support. Her reflections on this period highlight the intersection of personal grief and public life, as she continued to pursue her career and public responsibilities while coping with her loss.

In "Becoming," Michelle Obama shares the ways in which her father's memory continues to influence her life. She reflects on the lessons he taught her and the strength she draws from his example. His legacy of resilience and dedication to family remains a guiding force in her journey, providing a source of comfort and inspiration.

Michelle Obama's story offers a relatable and empathetic perspective on the experience of losing a parent. Her reflections on the enduring impact of her father's memory provide a sense of continuity and connection, illustrating that the bonds of love and family transcend physical absence. By sharing her journey, she offers a sense of companionship and understanding for those navigating similar losses.

Prince Harry and the Loss of Princess Diana

Prince Harry, Duke of Sussex, faced a highly publicized and deeply personal loss when his mother, Princess Diana, died in a tragic car accident in 1997. He was only twelve years old at the time, and the loss of his mother had a profound and lasting impact on his life. Prince Harry has spoken openly about his grief and the challenges of growing up without his mother's presence.

Princess Diana was a beloved figure known for her compassion, humanitarian efforts, and dedication to her children. Her sudden death left the world in shock and plunged her family into deep mourning. For Prince Harry, the loss was not only a personal tragedy but also a public event, as the eyes of the world were upon him and his family.

In the years following his mother's death, Prince Harry struggled with the weight of his grief and the expectations placed upon him as a member of the royal family. He has described feeling lost and overwhelmed, grappling with his emotions in the public eye. His journey through grief was marked by a period of emotional turmoil, during which he sought to find his path and identity.

Prince Harry's willingness to speak openly about his mental health and grief has been a powerful force for change. He has advocated for increased awareness and support for mental health issues, emphasizing the importance of seeking help and breaking the stigma around mental health struggles. His work with organizations such as Heads Together and the Invictus Games has highlighted the need for compassion and support for those facing similar challenges.

In interviews and public statements, Prince Harry has shared the impact of his mother's memory on his life. He has described how her legacy of compassion and service continues to inspire him and shape his work. By honouring her memory through his charitable efforts, he finds a sense of connection and purpose.

Prince Harry's story offers a poignant reminder of the enduring impact of grief and the importance of seeking support. His openness about his struggles and his dedication to helping others navigate their own grief journeys provide a sense of solidarity and hope for those facing similar losses.

Sheryl Sandberg and "Option B"

Sheryl Sandberg, COO of Facebook and author of "Lean In," faced an unexpected and devastating loss when her husband, Dave Goldberg, died suddenly in 2015. In her book "Option B: Facing Adversity, Building Resilience, and Finding Joy," co-authored with psychologist Adam Grant, Sandberg shares her journey through grief and the process of rebuilding her life after loss.

Dave Goldberg's death was a profound shock to Sheryl Sandberg and their family. Sandberg describes the immediate aftermath of his death as a period of intense sorrow and disbelief. She grappled with the sudden absence of her partner and the challenge of raising their two young children without him.

In "Option B," Sandberg reflects on the ways in which she navigated her grief and found resilience in the face of adversity. She emphasizes the importance of acknowledging and accepting the pain of loss while also seeking ways to rebuild and find moments of joy. Her journey involved leaning on her support network, seeking therapy, and finding strength in the memory of her husband's love and support.

One of the key themes in "Option B" is the concept of "post-traumatic growth," the idea that individuals can find new meaning and purpose in the aftermath of tragedy. Sandberg shares stories of others who have faced significant adversity and emerged with a renewed sense of purpose. Her reflections highlight the potential for growth and transformation that can arise from the process of navigating grief.

Sandberg's willingness to share her vulnerability and struggles offers a relatable and empathetic perspective on grief. Her emphasis on resilience, support, and finding meaning provides valuable insights for those navigating their own grief journeys. By sharing her story, she offers a sense of hope and encouragement for others facing similar challenges.

Patton Oswalt and the Loss of His Wife

Comedian and actor Patton Oswalt faced a profound and unexpected loss when his wife, Michelle McNamara, died suddenly in 2016. McNamara, a true crime writer, passed away in her sleep, leaving Oswalt and their young daughter to navigate life without her. Oswalt has been open about his grief journey, sharing his experiences through interviews, social media, and his stand-up comedy.

Michelle McNamara's death was a devastating blow to Patton Oswalt. He described the immediate aftermath as a period of numbness and disbelief, struggling to comprehend the sudden loss of his wife. Oswalt faced the challenge of supporting their daughter while coping with his own grief, a process he has described as both heartbreaking and transformative.

In the months following McNamara's death, Oswalt found solace in completing her unfinished book, "I'll Be Gone in the Dark," a true crime investigation into the Golden State Killer. By dedicating himself to finishing her work, he found a way to honour her memory and keep her legacy alive. The book's eventual publication and success provided a sense of closure and fulfilment.

Oswalt has been candid about the complexities of grief, describing the oscillation between moments of deep sorrow and fleeting glimpses of hope. His reflections on the grieving process highlight the importance of allowing oneself to feel and express a wide range of emotions, from anger and despair to joy and gratitude.

Through his stand-up comedy, Oswalt has also used

humour as a coping mechanism, finding ways to laugh and find moments of light amidst the darkness. His willingness to share his grief journey with audiences offers a sense of connection and understanding, reminding others that it is possible to find moments of joy and resilience even in the midst of profound loss.

Patton Oswalt's story underscores the importance of honouring the memory of a loved one and finding ways to move forward while acknowledging the pain of loss. His openness about his grief journey provides a sense of companionship and hope for others navigating similar challenges.

Viola Davis and Overcoming Childhood Trauma

Viola Davis, an acclaimed actress and producer, has spoken openly about the trauma and grief she experienced during her childhood. Growing up in poverty and facing numerous hardships, Davis's journey of overcoming adversity is both inspiring and deeply moving. Her story highlights the impact of childhood grief and the resilience required to heal and thrive.

Viola Davis was born into a family struggling with poverty in South Carolina. Her early years were marked by instability, hunger, and exposure to violence. These experiences left a lasting impact on Davis, shaping her understanding of the world and her place in it. Despite the challenges she faced, Davis found solace in storytelling and acting, which became a means of escape and self-expression.

Davis has shared that one of the most significant sources of grief in her life was the loss of her childhood innocence and the trauma of growing up in a violent and unstable environment. She described the pain of feeling unseen and unprotected, which fuelled her determination to create a better future for herself.

In her memoir "Finding Me," Davis reflects on the journey of healing and self-discovery. She emphasizes the importance of acknowledging and confronting the pain of the past to find healing and empowerment. Through therapy, self-reflection, and creative expression, Davis was able to navigate her grief and transform it into a source of strength.

One of the key themes in Davis's story is the power of resilience and the ability to rise above adversity. She has spoken about the importance of finding one's voice and embracing one's identity, despite the challenges and pain of the past. Her journey is a testament to the transformative power of self-acceptance and determination.

Viola Davis's story offers a powerful example of overcoming childhood grief and trauma. Her reflections on healing and resilience provide valuable insights for others facing similar challenges. By sharing her journey, Davis offers a sense of hope and inspiration, reminding others that it is possible to find strength and purpose in the face of adversity.

Queen Elizabeth II and the Loss of Prince Philip

Queen Elizabeth II, the longest-reigning British monarch, faced a profound personal loss when her husband, Prince Philip, Duke of Edinburgh, passed away in April 2021. Their marriage, which lasted over 73 years, was a cornerstone of her life and reign. The loss of Prince Philip marked the end of an era for the Queen and the British royal family.

Prince Philip's death was a significant moment in British history, and the public mourning was extensive. For Queen Elizabeth, the loss was deeply personal. Prince Philip had been her constant companion and support throughout her reign, offering guidance and unwavering loyalty. His absence left a significant void in her life.

In the days following Prince Philip's death, the Queen displayed her characteristic stoicism and dedication to duty. She continued to fulfil her public responsibilities, embodying the resilience and strength that have defined her reign. However, those close to her noted the profound grief she felt and the adjustments she had to make in her daily life.

The Queen's reflections on her husband's death were evident in her public statements and actions. She described Prince Philip as her "strength and stay," acknowledging the deep bond they shared and the impact of his loss on her life. The subdued and respectful nature of his funeral, influenced by the COVID-19 pandemic, allowed for a more intimate and personal farewell.

Queen Elizabeth's journey through grief is marked by her commitment to her role and the support of her family and the nation. Her ability to balance personal sorrow with public duty serves as an example of resilience and dedication. Her story highlights the universal nature of grief and how individuals navigate loss while continuing to fulfil their responsibilities.

By sharing her experiences and reflections, Queen Elizabeth II offers a sense of solidarity and understanding for those navigating their own grief journeys. Her story underscores the importance of finding strength in the community and the enduring impact of love and companionship.

J.K. Rowling and the Loss of Her Mother

J.K. Rowling, the author of the beloved Harry Potter series, experienced profound grief following the death of her mother, Anne Rowling. Her mother's passing had a significant impact on her life and writing, influencing the themes and emotional depth of her work. Rowling's journey through grief and the creative process offers a compelling exploration of how loss can shape one's artistic expression.

Anne Rowling died in December 1990 after a long battle with multiple sclerosis. Her death occurred just as J.K. Rowling was beginning to develop the concept for the Harry Potter series. The loss of her mother was a devastating blow, leaving Rowling grappling with intense sorrow and the challenge of finding direction in her life.

Rowling has spoken about how her mother's death influenced the creation of the Harry Potter series. The themes of loss, love, and resilience are woven throughout the books, reflecting Rowling's own experiences with grief. The character of Harry Potter, who is orphaned and must navigate the complexities of life without his parents, embodies the sense of loss and the search for identity that Rowling felt.

Writing became a therapeutic outlet for Rowling, allowing her to process her emotions and find a sense of purpose. The act of creating a magical world where love and friendship triumph over darkness provided her with a way to honour her mother's memory and explore the impact of loss. Rowling has described the process of writing as a means of healing and self-discovery.

In interviews, Rowling has shared the emotional journey of bringing the Harry Potter series to life. She described the moments of doubt and despair, as well as the joy and fulfilment of seeing her work resonate with readers around the world. Her story highlights the transformative power of creativity and the ways in which grief can inspire profound artistic expression.

J.K. Rowling's story offers a poignant example of how personal loss can shape one's creative work and lead to new forms of expression. Her reflections on grief and the creative process provide valuable insights for others navigating similar experiences. By sharing her journey, Rowling offers a sense of connection and understanding, reminding others of the healing power of storytelling and artistic expression.

Joe Biden and the Loss of His Son, Beau

President Joe Biden has faced multiple profound losses in his life, including the death of his son, Beau Biden, in 2015. Beau, who was an attorney and the former Attorney General of Delaware, died from brain cancer at the age of 46. The loss of Beau had a significant impact on Joe Biden and his family, shaping his perspectives on grief, resilience, and public service.

Beau Biden's death was a devastating blow to Joe Biden, who had already experienced the loss of his first wife and daughter in a car accident in 1972. The grief of losing Beau, who was a source of pride and hope for the Biden family, brought immense sorrow. Joe Biden has often spoken about the deep bond he shared with Beau and the pain of losing a beloved son.

In his memoir "Promise Me, Dad: A Year of Hope, Hardship, and Purpose," Joe Biden reflects on the year following Beau's diagnosis and death. He describes the emotional journey of navigating his grief while continuing to fulfil his responsibilities as Vice President. The memoir offers an intimate look at the impact of Beau's death on Biden's personal and professional life.

One of the key themes in Biden's reflections is the importance of family and community in the grieving process. He emphasizes the support he received from his family, friends, and colleagues, which provided him with the strength to move forward. Biden's story highlights the significance of leaning on loved ones and finding solace in shared memories and connections.

Biden has also spoken about the role of faith in his

journey through grief. His Catholic faith provided him with a sense of hope and comfort, helping him navigate the darkest moments of his loss. Biden's reflections on faith and resilience offer valuable insights for others seeking to find meaning and strength in the face of adversity.

Joe Biden's story is a testament to the power of resilience and the enduring impact of love and family. His willingness to share his experiences with grief provides a sense of solidarity and hope for others facing similar challenges. By reflecting on his journey, Biden offers a model of courage and compassion, reminding others that it is possible to find moments of joy and purpose amidst profound loss.

Robin Roberts and the Loss of Her Mother

Robin Roberts, the co-anchor of ABC's "Good Morning America," faced a profound personal loss when her mother, Lucimarian Tolliver Roberts, passed away in 2012. Lucimarian's death came at a particularly challenging time for Robin, who was undergoing treatment for myelodysplastic syndrome (MDS), a rare blood disorder. The loss of her mother had a significant impact on Robin's life, both personally and professionally.

Lucimarian Tolliver Roberts was a source of strength and inspiration for Robin. As the first African American to head Mississippi's Board of Education, Lucimarian was a trailblazer and a role model for her daughter. Her death left a significant void in Robin's life, especially as she navigated her own health challenges.

Robin has spoken openly about the impact of her mother's death on her journey through illness and recovery. She described the pain of not having her mother's physical presence during such a difficult time, but also the comfort she found in her mother's enduring spirit and love. Robin's reflections on her mother's influence highlight the importance of honouring the legacy of loved ones and finding strength in their memory.

In her memoir "Everybody's Got Something," Robin shares her experiences with grief and resilience. She reflects on the lessons she learned from her mother and how those lessons helped her navigate the challenges of life and illness. Robin's story emphasizes the importance of finding hope and purpose in the face of adversity.

Robin Roberts's willingness to share her journey through grief provides valuable insights and inspiration for others facing similar losses. Her reflections on the enduring impact of her mother's love and the power of resilience offer a sense of connection and hope. By sharing her story, Robin reminds others that it is possible to find strength and meaning amidst the pain of loss.

CHAPTER 4: THE IMPACT OF GRIEF

Physical Impact

Grief is not only an emotional and psychological experience but also a profoundly physical one. The body often bears the brunt of intense sorrow, manifesting in various physical symptoms and ailments that can affect one's overall health and well-being. Understanding the physical impact of grief is crucial for recognizing the importance of self-care and seeking appropriate support during the grieving process.

One of the most common physical symptoms of grief is fatigue. The emotional toll of loss can drain one's energy, leaving individuals feeling constantly tired and lethargic. This fatigue can be both mental and physical, making it difficult to perform even the simplest daily tasks. Sleep disturbances are also prevalent during grief, with many individuals experiencing insomnia or disrupted sleep patterns. The mind's constant processing of grief can make it hard to fall asleep or stay asleep, leading to a vicious cycle of exhaustion and emotional distress.

Changes in appetite are another common physical manifestation of grief. Some individuals may lose their appetite entirely, struggling to find the motivation to eat, while others might turn to food for comfort, leading to overeating. These changes can result in significant weight loss or gain, further impacting one's physical health. It's essential to be mindful of these shifts and strive for a balanced diet, even when it feels challenging.

Grief can also weaken the immune system, making individuals more susceptible to illnesses and infections. The stress and emotional strain associated with grief can reduce the body's ability to fight off common ailments, leading to an increase in colds, flu, and other health issues. This susceptibility underscores the importance of self-care and seeking medical attention when needed during the grieving process.

The cardiovascular system is another area that can be significantly affected by grief. Intense emotional stress can lead to elevated blood pressure, heart palpitations, and even an increased risk of heart attack. This phenomenon, sometimes referred to as "broken heart syndrome" or stress-induced cardiomyopathy, highlights the profound connection between emotional and physical health. It is essential for individuals experiencing severe physical symptoms to consult with healthcare professionals to manage these risks.

In addition to these specific symptoms, grief can also exacerbate existing health conditions. For individuals with chronic illnesses or conditions, the added stress of grieving can worsen symptoms and complicate treatment. Managing these conditions alongside grief requires a comprehensive approach that addresses both physical and emotional needs.

Physical manifestations of grief can also include headaches, body aches, and gastrointestinal issues. Tension headaches and migraines can be triggered by the stress and emotional turmoil of grief, while muscle aches and joint pain can result from physical tension and fatigue. Gastrointestinal issues, such as stomach aches, nausea, and digestive problems, are also common, reflecting the body's response to stress and anxiety.

Recognizing the physical impact of grief is the first step toward addressing these symptoms and promoting overall well-being. Self-care practices, such as maintaining a balanced diet, engaging in regular physical activity, and ensuring adequate rest, are crucial for supporting the body during this time. Gentle exercises, such as walking, yoga, or stretching, can help alleviate physical tension and promote relaxation.

Mindfulness and relaxation techniques can also be beneficial for managing the physical symptoms of grief. Practices such as deep breathing, meditation, and progressive muscle relaxation can reduce stress and promote a sense of calm. These techniques can help individuals connect with their bodies and become more attuned to their physical needs.

Seeking professional support is also important for addressing the physical impact of grief. Healthcare providers, including primary care physicians, mental health professionals, and grief counsellors, can offer valuable guidance and support. They can help individuals manage their physical symptoms, provide recommendations for self-care, and offer interventions to address specific health concerns.

Support groups and community resources can also play a vital role in managing the physical impact of grief. Connecting with others who are experiencing similar challenges can provide a sense of solidarity and encouragement. Sharing experiences and coping strategies can help individuals feel less alone and more empowered to take care of their physical health.

Ultimately, acknowledging and addressing the physical impact of grief is essential for holistic healing. By taking care of their bodies, individuals can support their overall well-being and resilience during the grieving process. This comprehensive approach to grief can help individuals navigate their journey with greater strength and hope.

Emotional Impact

The emotional impact of grief is profound and multifaceted, affecting every aspect of an individual's inner world. Grief is an intense emotional response to loss, encompassing a wide range of feelings that can be overwhelming and difficult to manage. Understanding the emotional impact of grief is essential for recognizing the depth of the experience and finding ways to cope and heal.

One of the most pervasive emotions associated with grief is sadness. This deep, pervasive feeling can permeate every moment of daily life, creating a sense of emptiness and despair. Sadness in grief is not merely a fleeting feeling but a profound sense of loss that can be all-encompassing. It is often accompanied by crying, emotional numbness, and a longing for the lost person or thing.

Anger is another common emotional response to grief. This anger can be directed at various targets, including oneself, others, or the circumstances surrounding the loss. Individuals may feel angry at the perceived unfairness of the loss, at themselves for not preventing it, or at others who they believe could have done more. Anger can be a way of expressing the deep pain and frustration that comes with loss.

Guilt is an emotion that many people experience during grief. They may feel responsible for the loss or believe that they could have done something to prevent it. This guilt can be irrational and unfounded, yet it is a powerful and often debilitating emotion. Individuals may replay events in their minds, searching for ways they could have acted differently.

Fear is also a significant part of the emotional landscape of grief. The loss of a loved one can create a sense of vulnerability and uncertainty about the future. Individuals may worry about their ability to cope without the person or thing they have lost, fear further losses, or feel anxious about their changed circumstances. This fear can lead to a heightened sense of insecurity and anxiety.

Loneliness is another common emotional experience in grief. The absence of a significant person or thing can create a profound sense of isolation and disconnection. Individuals may feel that no one truly understands their pain or that they are alone in their suffering. This loneliness can be exacerbated by changes in social dynamics and support systems.

The emotional impact of grief also includes confusion and disorientation. The loss can disrupt an individual's sense of reality and order, leading to feelings of bewilderment and instability. They may find it difficult to concentrate, make decisions, or carry out daily activities. This cognitive disruption is a normal part of the grieving process, reflecting the profound impact of the loss on one's mental and emotional functioning.

Hopelessness and despair can also accompany grief, especially in the face of significant or traumatic loss. Individuals may struggle to find meaning or purpose in life without the presence of their loved one or cherished thing. This sense of hopelessness can lead to a lack of motivation and a withdrawal from activities that once brought joy and fulfilment.

It is important to recognize that these emotional responses are natural and valid parts of the grieving process. Each person's grief journey is unique, and there is no "right" way to feel or express grief. The intensity and duration of these emotions can vary widely, and individuals may experience them in different ways and at different times.

Coping with the emotional impact of grief requires self-compassion and patience. Allowing oneself to feel and express these emotions without judgment is crucial for healing. This might involve crying, talking about the loss, writing in a journal, or engaging in creative activities that provide an outlet for emotional expression.

Seeking support from others can also be immensely helpful. Sharing one's feelings with trusted friends, family members, or support groups can provide validation and comfort. These connections can help individuals feel understood and less alone in their grief. Professional support from therapists or grief counsellors can offer additional guidance and tools for managing intense emotions.

Engaging in self-care practices is essential for emotional well-being during grief. This might include physical activities, mindfulness and relaxation techniques, hobbies, and spending time in nature. These activities can provide a sense of balance and stability, helping individuals navigate the ups and downs of their emotional journey.

Spiritual or religious practices can also provide comfort and solace for those who find meaning in them. Prayer, meditation, and participation in religious or spiritual communities can offer a sense of connection, purpose, and hope. These practices can help individuals find a sense of peace and acceptance, even in the face of profound loss.

Ultimately, the emotional impact of grief is a testament to the depth of our connections and the significance of our losses. By acknowledging and honouring these emotions, individuals can find a path toward healing and growth. Grief is not something to be "fixed" or "overcome," but a process to be experienced and integrated into one's life. With time, support, and self-compassion, it is possible to find a way to live with the loss and to carry the memory of the loved one or cherished thing forward in a meaningful and life-affirming way.

Mental Impact

Grief profoundly affects not only our emotions and physical health but also our mental and cognitive functioning. The mental impact of grief can be challenging to navigate, as it often involves disruptions in thought processes, concentration, memory, and overall cognitive abilities. Understanding these mental effects is crucial for managing grief and finding effective coping strategies.

One of the most common mental impacts of grief is difficulty concentrating. Individuals may find it hard to focus on tasks, follow conversations, or engage in activities that require sustained attention. This lack of concentration can affect work, school, and daily responsibilities, leading to feelings of frustration and inefficiency. The mind's preoccupation with the loss and the emotions associated with it can make it challenging to stay present and engaged in the moment.

Memory lapses are another frequent cognitive symptom of grief. People may struggle to remember details, appointments, or tasks, and they might find themselves forgetting things they would typically remember easily. This forgetfulness can be distressing, especially for those who rely on their memory for their personal and professional lives. It is important to understand that these memory issues are a normal part of the grieving process and often improve over time.

Grief can also lead to rumination, where individuals become preoccupied with thoughts about the loss, the circumstances surrounding it, and their feelings of guilt or regret. This repetitive thinking can create a mental loop that is difficult to break, making it hard to move forward. Rumination can exacerbate feelings of sadness, anger, and guilt, and it can contribute to mental exhaustion.

Confusion and a sense of disorientation are also common mental impacts of grief. The loss of a loved one or a significant part of one's life can disrupt the established order and routines, leading to a sense of chaos and instability. Individuals may feel uncertain about their future, question their beliefs and values, and struggle to find a sense of direction. This mental disarray can be disconcerting and overwhelming.

Grief can also impact decision-making abilities. The cognitive load of processing grief can make it challenging to make decisions, both big and small. Individuals may feel indecisive, second-guess their choices, or avoid making decisions altogether. This can affect various aspects of life, from everyday activities to significant life changes.

Intrusive thoughts are another mental challenge associated with grief. These are unwelcome and distressing thoughts that can suddenly appear, often related to the loss or the deceased. They can be vivid and disturbing, causing additional emotional pain and anxiety. Managing intrusive thoughts requires strategies to refocus the mind and find ways to cope with the distress they cause.

Someone who has lost a sibling might constantly replay the moments leading up to their death, wondering if they could have done something to prevent it. These intrusive thoughts can disrupt their daily life and make it difficult to find peace.

The mental impact of grief can also manifest as anxiety. Individuals may experience heightened worry and fear about the future, their own health, or the well-being of other loved ones. This anxiety can be pervasive and impact one's ability to relax and feel secure. It is important to address these feelings of anxiety and seek support to manage them effectively.

To navigate the mental impact of grief, it is essential to employ coping strategies and seek support. Here are some effective approaches:

1. Mindfulness and Meditation: Practices such as mindfulness meditation can help individuals stay present and reduce the mental clutter associated with grief. Mindfulness encourages a non-judgmental awareness of one's thoughts and feelings, which can help manage rumination and intrusive thoughts.

2. Journaling: Writing about one's thoughts and feelings can provide an outlet for processing grief. Journaling can help clarify emotions, reduce mental overload, and offer insights into one's grief journey.

3. Cognitive Behavioural Techniques: Cognitive-behavioural strategies can help individuals identify and challenge negative thought patterns related to grief. Techniques such as cognitive restructuring can assist in reframing thoughts and reducing the impact of rumination.

4. Engaging in Routine and Structure: Establishing a daily routine and structure can provide a sense of stability

and normalcy. Even simple activities like setting regular mealtimes, exercise, and hobbies can help manage the mental chaos of grief.

5. Physical Activity: Regular physical exercise has been shown to improve cognitive function and reduce symptoms of anxiety and depression. Activities such as walking, yoga, or swimming can provide both physical and mental benefits.

6. Professional Support: Seeking help from mental health professionals, such as therapists or grief counsellors, can provide valuable tools and support for managing the mental impact of grief. Therapy can offer a safe space to explore thoughts and feelings and develop effective coping strategies.

7. Social Support: Connecting with others who have experienced similar losses can provide validation and understanding. Support groups and community resources can offer a sense of belonging and reduce feelings of isolation.

By employing these strategies and seeking appropriate support, individuals can navigate the mental impact of grief more effectively. It is important to remember that the cognitive challenges associated with grief are a natural response to loss and that with time and effort, it is possible to regain a sense of mental clarity and balance.

Social Impact

The social impact of grief extends beyond the individual, affecting relationships, social interactions, and one's overall sense of community and belonging. Grieving can alter the dynamics of personal and professional relationships, leading to feelings of isolation, misunderstandings, and changes in social roles. Understanding these social effects is crucial for fostering supportive environments and maintaining meaningful connections during the grieving process.

One of the most immediate social impacts of grief is the feeling of isolation. The intense emotions and personal nature of grief can make it difficult to relate to others, leading individuals to withdraw from social activities and interactions. They may feel that others do not understand their pain or that their grief is too overwhelming to share. This isolation can compound the sense of loneliness and make it harder to find support.

A lady who loses her husband might feel unable to participate in social gatherings where couples are present, fearing that she will feel out of place or that her presence will dampen the mood. This withdrawal can lead to a sense of disconnection from her social network, further intensifying her grief.

Grief can also strain personal relationships. Friends and family members may struggle to know how to support a grieving person, leading to awkwardness or avoidance. Some might offer well-meaning but unhelpful advice, while others might withdraw out of discomfort or fear of saying the wrong thing. These reactions can create misunderstandings and tension, making the grieving person feel unsupported and alone.

Those supporting a grieving individual need to offer a compassionate and non-judgmental presence. Listening actively, validating their feelings, and being patient can help maintain and strengthen relationships during this challenging time. Offering practical support, such as helping with daily tasks or simply being present, can also make a significant difference.

The social impact of grief can also extend to professional relationships and the workplace. Grieving individuals may find it difficult to concentrate on work, meet deadlines, or engage in professional interactions. Colleagues and supervisors may not understand the depth of their grief or may lack the knowledge on how to provide appropriate support. This can lead to decreased productivity, tension in the workplace, and potential job insecurity.

Employers can play a crucial role in supporting grieving employees by offering flexible work arrangements, providing access to counselling services, and fostering a compassionate work environment. Open communication and understanding from colleagues can help create a supportive atmosphere that acknowledges the challenges of grief while promoting a sense of community.

Grief can also impact one's social roles and responsibilities. The loss of a loved one can lead to changes in family dynamics, caregiving responsibilities, and social identities. Imagine the death of a spouse may require the surviving partner to take on new roles, such as managing household finances or caring for children alone. These changes can be overwhelming and require significant adjustment.

Support from family members, friends, and community resources can help ease these transitions. Practical assistance, emotional support, and access to resources such as counselling or support groups can provide valuable help during this time of change.

Cultural and societal expectations around grief can also influence its social impact. Different cultures have varying norms and rituals for mourning, which can affect how individuals express their grief and seek support. In some cultures, public displays of mourning are encouraged, while in others, grief is considered a private matter. Understanding and respecting these cultural differences is important for providing appropriate support and fostering a sense of community.

Social support networks, including friends, family, community organizations, and support groups, play a vital role in helping individuals navigate the social impact of grief. These networks can provide a sense of belonging, validation, and practical assistance. Connecting with others who have experienced similar losses can offer comfort and reduce feelings of isolation.

Think about a man who loses his best friend might find solace in joining a bereavement support group. Sharing his experiences with others who understand his pain can provide validation and a sense of community. These connections can help him feel less alone and more supported in his grieving journey.

Creating and maintaining social connections is essential for coping with the social impact of grief. While it can be challenging to reach out and engage with others during this time, it is important to remember that support and understanding are available. By fostering compassionate and supportive environments, individuals and communities can help those who are grieving feel understood, valued, and connected.

Personal Story - Ahmed's Struggle

Ahmed sat in his living room, staring at the empty chair where his father used to sit. It had been six months since his father passed away, but the pain still felt fresh, a constant ache that refused to fade. Ahmed's father had been his rock, a source of wisdom, strength, and unwavering support. Losing him felt like losing a part of himself, a wound that no time or distance could heal.

In the initial days after his father's death, Ahmed was surrounded by family and friends offering their condolences and support. The house was filled with people, the air thick with the sound of shared sorrow and whispered memories. But as the days turned into weeks, the visitors became fewer, and the house grew quieter. Ahmed was left alone with his grief, struggling to navigate a world that no longer made sense.

Ahmed's father had been a prominent figure in their community, a respected leader and a compassionate mentor. His death left a void not only in Ahmed's life but in the lives of many others. The pressure to live up to his father's legacy weighed heavily on Ahmed's shoulders. He felt an immense responsibility to carry forward his father's work, but he also felt utterly unprepared and overwhelmed.

The weight of his grief impacted every aspect of Ahmed's life. At work, he found it difficult to concentrate, his mind constantly drifting back to memories of his father. Simple tasks that he once performed effortlessly now seemed insurmountable. His colleagues tried to be supportive, but Ahmed could sense their impatience and frustration. He felt like a burden, a shadow of his former self.

Socially, Ahmed withdrew from his friends. He avoided gatherings and events, unable to face the questions and pitying looks. He didn't want to burden others with his pain, nor did he want to pretend that everything was okay. His isolation grew, and with it, a profound sense of loneliness. He missed the camaraderie and support of his friends, but he didn't know how to reach out.

At home, the silence was deafening. The rituals and routines that had once brought comfort now felt hollow. The sight of his father's belongings, untouched and gathering dust, brought a fresh wave of pain each time. Ahmed often found himself sitting in his father's chair, hoping to feel some connection, some semblance of the warmth and wisdom that had once filled the room.

The community that had once rallied around Ahmed and his family also seemed to move on. The initial outpouring of support dwindled, and life returned to its usual rhythm. Ahmed felt forgotten, as if his grief was no longer valid or significant. He struggled with feelings of resentment and anger, questioning why life had to continue while he was still mired in sorrow.

Desperate for some relief, Ahmed decided to seek professional help. He found a grief counsellor who specialized in helping individuals cope with significant losses. In their sessions, Ahmed was encouraged to express his emotions and explore his feelings of guilt, anger, and sadness. The counsellor provided a safe and non-judgmental space where Ahmed could begin to process his grief.

Through therapy, Ahmed learned that his feelings were normal and valid. He was reminded that grief is not a linear process and that it was okay to experience a range of emotions. The counsellor also helped Ahmed develop coping strategies, such as mindfulness practices, journaling, and setting small, achievable goals. These tools provided Ahmed with a sense of control and helped him navigate the overwhelming tide of emotions.

Ahmed also started attending a local support group for individuals who had lost loved ones. Sharing his story with others who understood his pain provided a sense of validation and connection. He found solace in the collective experience of the group, realizing that he was not alone in his struggle. The support group became a lifeline, a place where he could find empathy, understanding, and hope.

Gradually, Ahmed began to re-engage with life. He reached out to his friends, explaining his need for space and his desire for their support. His friends responded with compassion and patience, giving him the time and space he needed while also encouraging him to join them in social activities. These connections helped Ahmed feel less isolated and more supported.

At work, Ahmed spoke with his supervisor about his struggles. They worked together to create a more flexible schedule, allowing Ahmed to manage his workload and take time for self-care. This accommodation reduced his stress and helped him regain a sense of balance.

Ahmed also found ways to honour his father's memory.

He started a scholarship fund in his father's name, supporting young students in their educational pursuits. This initiative provided Ahmed with a sense of purpose and fulfilment, allowing him to carry forward his father's legacy in a meaningful way.

While the pain of his loss never completely disappeared, Ahmed learned to live with it. He discovered that grief could coexist with hope and that he could find joy and meaning even in the face of profound sorrow. His journey through grief was far from over, but he had found the strength and resilience to continue moving forward.

Ahmed's struggle and eventual healing highlight the importance of seeking support, acknowledging one's emotions, and finding ways to honour and remember those we have lost. His story serves as a testament to the power of community, compassion, and the human spirit's capacity for resilience.

CHAPTER 5: THE CHALLENGES OF GRIEF

Facing the Unknown

One of the most daunting challenges of grief is facing the unknown. The loss of a loved one or a significant part of one's life often leaves individuals feeling unmoored, adrift in a sea of uncertainty. The future, once predictable and secure, now appears filled with questions and fears. This uncertainty can be a significant source of anxiety and stress, making it difficult to move forward.

Grief often disrupts the established order of life, leading to changes in routines, roles, and relationships. The unknown can manifest in various ways, such as financial instability, changes in family dynamics, or the loss of a sense of identity. Navigating these changes requires resilience and adaptability, but it can also be incredibly challenging.

Imagine the death of a spouse can leave the surviving partner grappling with numerous unknowns. They may worry about how to manage finances, maintain the household, and provide for their family. The loss of companionship and support can create a void that feels impossible to fill, leaving them questioning their ability to cope on their own.

Facing the unknown also involves confronting existential questions about the meaning and purpose of life. The loss of a loved one can lead individuals to question their beliefs, values, and place in the world. This existential crisis can be unsettling, adding to the emotional and mental strain of grief.

One way to navigate the unknown is to focus on the present moment. Mindfulness practices, such as meditation and deep breathing, can help individuals stay grounded and reduce anxiety about the future. By focusing on what can be controlled in the present, individuals can find a sense of stability and calm amidst the uncertainty.

Setting small, achievable goals can also provide a sense of direction and purpose. These goals can be as simple as getting out of bed, preparing a meal, or going for a walk. Accomplishing these tasks can build confidence and create a sense of progress, even in the face of overwhelming uncertainty.

Seeking support from others is crucial when facing the unknown. Friends, family members, and support groups can provide valuable insights, advice, and encouragement. Sharing fears and concerns with trusted individuals can reduce feelings of isolation and provide a broader perspective on potential solutions.

Think about a person who loses her job and faces financial uncertainty might find support from a career counsellor or financial advisor. These professionals can help her explore new career opportunities, develop a budget, and create a plan for financial stability. By seeking help, she can feel more empowered to navigate the unknown and take proactive steps toward her future.

Embracing change is another important aspect of facing the unknown. While change can be difficult and uncomfortable, it can also lead to growth and new opportunities. Viewing change as a potential for personal development and new experiences can shift the focus from fear to possibility.

Imagine a man who loses his ability to work due to a chronic illness might initially feel overwhelmed by the unknown future. However, by embracing change, he might discover new interests and passions, such as volunteering or pursuing a hobby. These new activities can provide a sense of purpose and fulfilment, helping him navigate the uncertainty with hope and resilience.

It is also important to acknowledge and validate one's fears and anxieties about the unknown. These feelings are natural and understandable, and it is okay to experience them. By accepting these emotions without judgment, individuals can reduce their intensity and begin to explore ways to manage them effectively.

Professional support, such as therapy or counselling, can provide valuable tools and strategies for coping with the unknown. Mental health professionals can help individuals identify their fears, develop coping mechanisms, and build resilience. Therapy can also offer a safe space to explore existential questions and find meaning in the face of loss.

Ultimately, facing the unknown is about finding a balance between acknowledging the uncertainty and taking proactive steps toward the future. It involves embracing change, seeking support, and focusing on the present moment. By navigating the unknown with resilience and adaptability, individuals can find a path forward and discover new possibilities for growth and fulfilment.

Dealing with Emotional Turmoil

The emotional turmoil of grief can be overwhelming and all-consuming, affecting every aspect of an individual's life. The intensity and complexity of emotions can create a sense of chaos and instability, making it difficult to find peace and balance. Dealing with this emotional turmoil requires understanding, compassion, and effective coping strategies.

Grief often brings a whirlwind of emotions, including sadness, anger, guilt, fear, and confusion. These emotions can fluctuate rapidly, leaving individuals feeling emotionally exhausted and unsure of how to navigate their feelings. It is important to recognize that this emotional turmoil is a natural response to loss and that it is okay to feel a wide range of emotions.

Sadness is one of the most pervasive emotions in grief. It can create a profound sense of emptiness and longing, as individuals mourn the absence of their loved one or cherished thing. This sadness can be intense and persistent, making it difficult to find joy or motivation. Allowing oneself to feel and express this sadness is crucial for processing grief and finding healing.

Anger is another common emotion in grief, often directed at oneself, others, or the circumstances surrounding the loss. Anger can provide a temporary sense of control and release, but it can also be destructive if not managed effectively. Finding healthy outlets for anger, such as physical activity or creative expression, can help reduce its intensity and prevent it from causing harm.

Guilt is a powerful emotion that can accompany grief, as individuals question their actions and decisions leading up to the loss. They may feel responsible for the loss or believe that they could have done something to prevent it. It is important to recognize that guilt is often irrational and unfounded and to practice self-compassion and forgiveness.

Fear and anxiety can also be significant parts of the emotional turmoil of grief. The loss of a loved one can create a sense of vulnerability and uncertainty about the future. Individuals may worry about their ability to cope, fear further losses, or feel anxious about their changed circumstances. Addressing these fears and seeking support can help reduce anxiety and provide a sense of security.

Confusion and disorientation are common cognitive symptoms of grief, reflecting the disruption and instability that loss can create. Individuals may find it difficult to concentrate, make decisions, or carry out daily activities. This mental fog can add to the emotional strain, making it important to find ways to manage cognitive symptoms and maintain a sense of order.

Coping with the emotional turmoil of grief involves several strategies:

1. Expressing Emotions: Allowing oneself to feel and express emotions without judgment is crucial for processing grief. This might involve talking to a trusted friend, writing in a journal, or engaging in creative activities like painting or music.

2. Seeking Support: Connecting with others who understand and empathize with one's grief can provide validation and comfort. Support groups, therapy, and community resources can offer valuable support and reduce feelings of isolation.

3. Practicing Self-Care: Engaging in activities that nurture and soothe the body and mind is essential for emotional well-being. This might include physical exercise, mindfulness and relaxation techniques, hobbies, and spending time in nature.

4. Setting Boundaries: Recognizing and respecting one's limits is important for managing emotional turmoil. This might involve setting boundaries with others, taking breaks from social activities, and allowing time for rest and solitude.

5. Mindfulness and Meditation: Practices such as mindfulness meditation can help individuals stay present and reduce the intensity of emotional fluctuations. Mindfulness encourages a non-judgmental awareness of one's thoughts and feelings, which can help manage emotional turmoil.

6. Professional Support: Seeking help from mental health

professionals can provide valuable tools and strategies for coping with intense emotions. Therapy can offer a safe space to explore and process feelings, develop coping mechanisms, and build resilience.

7. Creating Rituals: Engaging in rituals or activities that honour and remember the loved one can provide a sense of connection and continuity. This might include creating a memorial, participating in charity events, or establishing new traditions.

8. Focusing on the Present: Grounding oneself in the present moment can help reduce anxiety about the future and provide a sense of stability. Mindfulness practices, deep breathing, and grounding exercises can help individuals stay present and manage emotional fluctuations.

Imagine a woman who loses her child might find solace in creating a memorial garden. Tending to the garden provides a sense of purpose and a way to honour her child's memory. She also practices mindfulness meditation to stay grounded and reduce the intensity of her emotions.

Dealing with emotional turmoil is a journey that requires time, patience, and self-compassion. It is important to recognize that grief is a dynamic and evolving process and that it is okay to experience a wide range of emotions. By employing effective coping strategies and seeking support, individuals can navigate the emotional turmoil of grief and find a path toward healing and balance.

Social Isolation

Grief can often lead to social isolation, a state where

individuals feel disconnected from others and cut off from their usual social networks. This isolation can be both a result of the grieving person's withdrawal and the reactions of those around them. Understanding the causes and effects of social isolation during grief is essential for finding ways to reconnect and build supportive relationships.

When a significant loss occurs, the intensity of emotions can make it difficult for individuals to engage with others. They may feel that their grief is too overwhelming to share or that others do not understand their pain. This can lead to a withdrawal from social activities, gatherings, and interactions. The desire to avoid questions, pitying looks, or well-meaning but unhelpful advice can further contribute to isolation.

Imagine a person who loses his wife might find it painful to attend social events where couples are present. The sight of others enjoying their time together can intensify his feelings of loss and loneliness. To protect himself from this pain, he might choose to stay home, leading to a cycle of isolation and further emotional distress.

Social isolation can also result from the reactions of others. Friends and family members may feel uncomfortable or unsure of how to support the grieving person. They might avoid discussing the loss, change the subject, or distance themselves out of fear of saying the wrong thing. These reactions can make the grieving person feel misunderstood and unsupported, exacerbating their sense of isolation.

The impact of social isolation on a grieving individual can be profound. It can lead to increased feelings of loneliness, depression, and anxiety. The lack of social support can also make it more challenging to navigate the practical and emotional aspects of grief. Isolation can create a sense of being stuck, making it harder to move forward and find healing.

Addressing social isolation during grief involves several key strategies:

1. Reaching Out: Taking the initiative to connect with others, even when it feels difficult, is important for breaking the cycle of isolation. This might involve reaching out to friends, family members, or support groups. Sharing one's feelings and experiences can provide a sense of connection and validation.

2. Finding Supportive Communities: Joining a support group for individuals who have experienced similar losses can provide a sense of belonging and understanding. These groups offer a safe space to share emotions, receive support, and build new connections.

3. Communicating Needs: Being open and honest with friends and family about one's needs and feelings can help them understand how to provide support. This might involve asking for specific forms of assistance, such as a listening ear, help with daily tasks, or companionship.

4. Engaging in Social Activities: Gradually re-engaging in social activities and routines can help reduce feelings of isolation. This might involve attending community events, participating in hobbies, or volunteering. These activities can provide a sense of purpose and connection.

5. Seeking Professional Support: Therapists and grief

counsellors can offer valuable guidance and support for managing social isolation. They can help individuals develop strategies for reconnecting with others and navigating social interactions.

6. Practicing Self-Compassion: Recognizing that social isolation is a common experience in grief and being gentle with oneself is important. It is okay to take time to heal and to set boundaries with social interactions as needed.

7. Using Technology: In today's digital age, technology can be a valuable tool for maintaining social connections. Video calls, social media, and online support groups can provide a sense of connection and community, even when in-person interactions are not possible.

Think about a lady who loses her brother might find it difficult to engage with her usual social circle. By joining an online support group for siblings who have experienced loss, she can connect with others who understand her pain. These virtual interactions provide comfort and reduce her sense of isolation.

Friends and family members can also play a crucial role in reducing social isolation. Offering consistent support, checking in regularly, and being present can make a significant difference. Understanding that the grieving person might need space at times but also needs connection is important. Providing a balance of presence and patience can help the grieving person feel supported and valued.

Ultimately, addressing social isolation involves finding a balance between honouring one's need for solitude and seeking connection. It requires patience, effort, and the willingness to reach out and accept support. By taking steps to reconnect with others and build supportive relationships, individuals can reduce feelings of isolation and find a sense of community and belonging during their grief journey.

Managing Daily Life

Managing daily life during grief can be a significant challenge. The emotional and cognitive toll of grief can make it difficult to perform everyday tasks and responsibilities. Establishing routines and finding strategies to cope with these challenges are crucial for maintaining a sense of stability and control.

Grief can disrupt one's ability to concentrate, make decisions, and stay organized. The overwhelming emotions and mental fog associated with grief can make even simple tasks feel daunting. This can lead to a sense of frustration and helplessness, adding to the emotional burden.

One of the first steps in managing daily life during grief is to prioritize tasks. Identifying the most essential activities and focusing on those can help reduce the sense of being overwhelmed. It is okay to let go of non-essential tasks and permit oneself to take things one step at a time.

Imagine a person who has lost a loved one might prioritize tasks such as paying bills, preparing meals, and attending work or school. Non-essential activities, such as extensive cleaning or social engagements, can be deferred until they feel more manageable.

Creating a routine can also provide a sense of structure

and normalcy. Establishing regular times for meals, sleep, exercise, and other daily activities can help anchor the day and provide a sense of predictability. This routine can offer comfort and reduce the chaos that grief can bring.

Breaking tasks into smaller steps can make them feel more manageable. Instead of tackling a large project all at once, breaking it down into smaller, more achievable steps can reduce the sense of overwhelm. Think about if cleaning the house feels too daunting, focusing on one room or area at a time can make the task more approachable.

Setting realistic expectations is important for managing daily life during grief. It is okay to adjust one's expectations and recognize that productivity might be lower than usual. Being kind and patient with oneself and acknowledging the impact of grief can reduce feelings of guilt and frustration.

Seeking help from others is another crucial strategy. Friends, family members, and community resources can provide practical assistance with tasks such as childcare, meal preparation, and household chores. Accepting help can reduce the burden and allow more time for self-care and emotional processing.

Self-care is essential for maintaining physical and emotional well-being. Engaging in activities that nurture and soothe the body and mind, such as exercise, mindfulness practices, and hobbies, can provide a sense of balance and relief. Ensuring adequate rest, nutrition, and hydration is also important for managing daily life during grief.

Using reminders and organizational tools can help with memory and concentration issues. Setting alarms, making to-do lists, and using calendars can provide structure and support for managing tasks. These tools can help reduce the mental load and provide a sense of control.

Imagine a man who loses his partner might struggle with remembering appointments and tasks. By using a calendar app to set reminders and make lists, he can keep track of his responsibilities and reduce cognitive strain.

Taking breaks and allowing time for rest is important for managing the physical and emotional exhaustion that comes with grief. Giving oneself permission to take breaks, rest, and engage in relaxing activities can help replenish energy and reduce stress.

Mindfulness and relaxation techniques can also support daily functioning. Practices such as deep breathing, meditation, and progressive muscle relaxation can reduce anxiety and promote a sense of calm. These techniques can help individuals stay present and focused, making it easier to manage daily tasks.

Connecting with support networks can provide emotional and practical assistance. Friends, family, support groups, and professional counsellors can offer valuable support and guidance. Sharing one's experiences and seeking advice can provide new perspectives and solutions for managing daily life.

Think about a woman who lost her parent might find it helpful to join a support group for adult children who have lost parents. Through the group, she can share her struggles and receive practical tips for managing daily tasks and coping with grief.

Ultimately, managing daily life during grief involves finding a balance between responsibilities and self-care. It requires patience, flexibility, and the willingness to seek support. By prioritizing tasks, establishing routines, and using coping strategies, individuals can navigate the challenges of daily life and find a sense of stability and control amidst the turmoil of grief.

Personal Story - Mei Ling's Courage

Mei Ling sat by the window, watching the rain tap gently against the glass. It had been a year since her mother passed away, but the pain still felt as raw as the day it happened. Her mother had been her confidante, her source of strength and wisdom. Losing her felt like losing a part of herself, a wound that time seemed unable to heal.

In the months following her mother's death, Mei Ling struggled to find her footing. The weight of her grief was all-consuming, making it difficult to concentrate at work or find joy in her hobbies. She withdrew from her friends, unable to face their pitying looks and well-meaning but empty platitudes. The isolation deepened her sorrow, creating a vicious cycle that seemed impossible to break.

One evening, as Mei Ling sorted through her mother's belongings, she came across a journal her mother had kept. The pages were filled with reflections, memories, and advice—words of wisdom that Mei Ling desperately needed. She spent hours reading through the journal, finding comfort in her mother's voice and guidance.

Inspired by her mother's words, Mei Ling decided to make a change. She knew her mother would not want her to live in perpetual sorrow. Drawing on the strength her mother had always shown, Mei Ling began to take small steps toward healing.

She started by reconnecting with her friends. At first, it was difficult to open up about her grief, but she soon realized that sharing her pain helped lighten the load. Her friends, once unsure of how to help, became pillars of support. They listened without judgment, offered practical assistance, and reminded her that it was okay to grieve.

Mei Ling also sought professional help. She found a grief counsellor who provided a safe space to explore her emotions and develop coping strategies. Through therapy, Mei Ling learned to navigate the complex terrain of her grief. She practiced mindfulness and meditation, which helped her stay present and manage the overwhelming waves of sadness and anxiety.

To honour her mother's memory, Mei Ling decided to volunteer at a local community centre, a place her mother had loved. Helping others gave her a sense of purpose and fulfilment, and it brought her closer to her mother's spirit. She found joy in giving back to the community and discovered that helping others was a powerful way to heal her own heart.

One of the most significant steps in Mei Ling's healing journey was returning to her love of painting. Her mother had always encouraged her artistic pursuits, and painting became a way for Mei Ling to express her emotions and keep her mother's memory alive. She spent hours in her studio, creating vibrant pieces that reflected her journey through grief and healing.

Mei Ling also established new rituals to remember her mother. She created a small altar in her home, adorned with her mother's favourite flowers, photographs, and mementos. Each morning, she would light a candle and spend a few moments in quiet reflection, feeling her mother's presence and drawing strength from her memories.

Through these small but significant steps, Mei Ling began to find a new sense of normalcy. She learned to live with her grief, understanding that it was a part of her but not all of her. She embraced the support of her friends, found solace in her volunteer work, and reconnected with her passion for painting.

Mei Ling's journey through grief was not linear. There were days when the pain felt unbearable, and she questioned whether she would ever truly heal. But with courage and determination, she continued to move forward, honouring her mother's legacy and finding new ways to live a meaningful and fulfilling life.

Her story is a testament to the power of resilience and the importance of seeking support. Mei Ling's courage to face her grief, connect with others, and find purpose in the midst of sorrow illustrates the profound capacity of the human spirit to heal and grow. Through her journey, she discovered that while the pain of loss never completely disappears, it is possible to find hope, joy, and a renewed sense of self.

CHAPTER 6: COPING WITH GRIEF

Healthy Coping Mechanisms

Coping with grief is a deeply personal journey, and finding healthy ways to navigate this process is crucial for emotional and physical well-being. While grief can feel overwhelming, various strategies can help individuals manage their emotions, maintain stability, and gradually move towards healing. Here are some healthy coping mechanisms that can support this journey:

1. Allowing Yourself to Grieve: One of the most important steps in coping with grief is to allow yourself to feel and express your emotions. This means giving yourself permission to cry, feel sad, angry, or even numb. Grieving is not a sign of weakness; it is a natural and necessary part of healing. Trying to suppress or ignore your feelings can prolong the grieving process and lead to additional emotional and physical issues.

2. Seeking Social Support: Connecting with friends, family, and support groups can provide invaluable support during the grieving process. Sharing your

feelings with others who understand or have experienced similar losses can offer comfort and reduce feelings of isolation. It is important to reach out and let others know how they can support you, whether it's through listening, helping with daily tasks, or simply being present.

3. Engaging in Physical Activity: Regular physical activity can have numerous benefits for your emotional and physical health. Exercise releases endorphins, which are natural mood lifters, and can help reduce symptoms of depression and anxiety. Activities such as walking, jogging, yoga, or even gentle stretching can provide a sense of routine and help alleviate the physical tension that often accompanies grief.

4. Practicing Mindfulness and Meditation: Mindfulness and meditation can be powerful tools for coping with grief. These practices involve focusing on the present moment and accepting your emotions without judgment. Mindfulness can help reduce anxiety and stress, improve emotional regulation, and provide a sense of calm. Guided meditations, deep breathing exercises, and progressive muscle relaxation are all effective techniques for managing grief-related stress.

5. Maintaining a Balanced Diet: Eating a healthy, balanced diet is essential for physical and emotional well-being. Grief can impact your appetite and eating habits, leading to either overeating or loss of appetite. It is important to nourish your body with nutritious foods that provide energy and support overall health. Staying hydrated and avoiding excessive alcohol or caffeine consumption can also help maintain balance.

6. Creating a Routine: Establishing a daily routine can

provide a sense of normalcy and stability during the grieving process. Having a schedule for meals, exercise, sleep, and self-care activities can help structure your day and reduce feelings of chaos. This routine can also serve as a gentle reminder to take care of yourself, even when you are feeling overwhelmed by grief.

7. Expressing Your Emotions Creatively: Creative expression can be a therapeutic way to process and release emotions. Writing in a journal, creating art, playing music, or engaging in other forms of creative activities can help you explore your feelings and find a sense of relief. These activities provide an outlet for your emotions and can help you make sense of your grief.

8. Seeking Professional Help: Sometimes, the intensity of grief can feel too overwhelming to manage on your own. Seeking help from a mental health professional, such as a therapist or grief counsellor, can provide additional support and guidance. Therapy can offer a safe space to explore your feelings, develop coping strategies, and work through the challenges of grief.

9. Honouring Your Loved One's Memory: Finding ways to remember and honour your loved one can provide comfort and a sense of connection. This might involve creating a memorial, participating in activities that were meaningful to them, or simply sharing stories and memories with others. These acts of remembrance can help keep your loved one's memory alive and provide a source of solace.

10. Practicing Self-Compassion: Being kind and gentle with yourself during the grieving process is crucial. Recognize that grief is a natural response to loss and that

it is okay to have good days and bad days. Treat yourself with the same compassion and understanding that you would offer to a friend. Allow yourself time to heal and acknowledge that the grieving process is unique for everyone.

Imagine a woman who loses her father might find comfort in joining a support group for those who have lost parents. Through the group, she can share her experiences, receive support, and learn coping strategies from others who understand her pain. She also practices mindfulness meditation daily, which helps her stay grounded and manage her emotions.

By incorporating these healthy coping mechanisms, individuals can navigate the complex emotions of grief and find a path towards healing. While the pain of loss may never completely disappear, these strategies can help build resilience and provide a sense of hope and strength during the grieving process.

Seeking Support

Seeking support is a vital aspect of coping with grief. The journey through loss can be incredibly isolating, but connecting with others who understand and care can provide comfort, validation, and practical assistance. There are various sources of support available, each offering different forms of help and understanding. Here are some key avenues for seeking support during the grieving process:

1. Family and Friends: Your immediate circle of family and friends can be an important source of support. These

individuals know you well and can provide emotional comfort, practical help, and companionship. Sharing your feelings and experiences with them can foster a sense of connection and reduce feelings of isolation. It is important to communicate your needs clearly and let them know how they can support you best.

2. Support Groups: Grief support groups offer a safe space for individuals to share their experiences and connect with others who are going through similar losses. These groups provide a sense of community and understanding that can be incredibly validating. Support groups can be found through local community centres, hospitals, religious organizations, or online platforms. Participating in a support group can help you feel less alone and provide new perspectives on coping with grief.

3. Therapy and Counselling: Professional help from therapists or grief counsellors can offer specialized support and guidance. Therapists are trained to help individuals navigate the complex emotions and challenges of grief. Therapy sessions provide a confidential and non-judgmental space to explore your feelings, develop coping strategies, and work through any unresolved issues. Therapy can be particularly helpful for those experiencing complicated or prolonged grief.

4. Online Communities: In today's digital age, online support communities can be a valuable resource for those grieving. Websites, forums, and social media groups dedicated to grief support offer a platform to share experiences, seek advice, and connect with others around the world. Online communities provide the flexibility to seek support at any time and can be especially beneficial for those who may have difficulty accessing in-person

groups.

5. Religious and Spiritual Support: For many individuals, religious or spiritual beliefs play a significant role in coping with grief. Religious leaders, such as clergy members or spiritual counsellors, can provide guidance, comfort, and rituals that honour the deceased. Engaging in spiritual practices, attending services, or participating in faith-based support groups can offer solace and a sense of meaning during the grieving process.

6. Community Resources: Various community resources can provide practical and emotional support. Nonprofit organizations, hospices, and local agencies often offer grief support services, including counselling, support groups, and educational programs. These resources can provide valuable information and assistance tailored to the needs of those who are grieving.

7. Work and School Support: Employers and educational institutions can also play a role in supporting individuals through grief. Many workplaces and schools have policies and resources in place to help employees and students manage their responsibilities while coping with loss. This might include flexible schedules, leave options, counselling services, and support from supervisors or teachers. Communicating your needs to your employer or school can help create a supportive environment.

8. Books and Educational Materials: Reading books, articles, and educational materials about grief can provide insights, comfort, and practical advice. Many books written by grief experts or individuals who have experienced significant loss can offer guidance and validation. These resources can help you understand the

grieving process and provide tools for coping.

9. Crisis Hotlines: For those experiencing intense grief and emotional distress, crisis hotlines can provide immediate support. These hotlines are staffed by trained professionals who can offer counselling, resources, and referrals. They are available 24/7 and can be a crucial lifeline for those in need of urgent help.

10. Self-Help and Personal Development: Engaging in self-help and personal development activities can also support the grieving process. This might include practicing mindfulness, journaling, engaging in creative arts, or pursuing new interests and hobbies. These activities can provide a sense of purpose, help process emotions, and promote overall well-being.

Imagine a man who loses his sister might find solace in joining an online support group for siblings who have experienced loss. Through the group, he can share his story, receive empathy and advice, and build connections with others who understand his grief. He also seeks therapy to address his intense feelings of guilt and anger, finding professional guidance to navigate these emotions.

Seeking support is not a sign of weakness; it is a crucial step in the healing process. By reaching out and connecting with others, individuals can find the strength, comfort, and resources they need to navigate their grief journey. Support can come in many forms, and it is important to explore and utilize the options that best meet your needs.

Mindfulness and Meditation

Mindfulness and meditation are powerful tools for coping with grief. These practices involve focusing on the present moment, accepting your emotions without judgment, and cultivating a sense of calm and clarity. Integrating mindfulness and meditation into your daily routine can provide numerous benefits for emotional and physical well-being, helping you navigate the complexities of grief.

1. Understanding Mindfulness: Mindfulness is the practice of paying attention to the present moment with an open and non-judgmental attitude. It involves being fully aware of your thoughts, feelings, and physical sensations as they arise, without trying to change or avoid them. Mindfulness encourages acceptance and compassion towards yourself, which can be especially beneficial during the grieving process.

2. Benefits of Mindfulness for Grief: Practicing mindfulness can help reduce the intensity of grief-related emotions, such as sadness, anxiety, and anger. It can improve emotional regulation, enhance self-awareness, and promote a sense of inner peace. Mindfulness can also help you stay grounded in the present moment, reducing rumination and worry about the past or future.

3. Getting Started with Mindfulness: To begin practicing mindfulness, find a quiet and comfortable place where you can sit or lie down without distractions. Close your eyes and take a few deep breaths, focusing on the sensation of your breath as it enters and leaves your body. Allow yourself to become aware of your thoughts and emotions, observing them without judgment. If your

mind wanders, gently bring your focus back to your breath.

4. Guided Mindfulness Meditation: Guided mindfulness meditations can be a helpful way to start practicing mindfulness. These meditations are led by a guide or instructor who provides verbal instructions to help you stay focused and present. You can find guided mindfulness meditations through apps, websites, and online videos.

5. Body Scan Meditation: The body scan is a mindfulness practice that involves focusing on different parts of your body and observing any sensations you feel. Lie down or sit comfortably and close your eyes. Starting at your toes, slowly move your attention upward, noticing any tension, discomfort, or relaxation in each part of your body. This practice can help you become more aware of physical sensations and release tension.

6. Loving-Kindness Meditation: Loving-kindness meditation, also known as meta meditation, involves cultivating feelings of compassion and kindness towards yourself and others. Sit comfortably and close your eyes. Begin by silently repeating phrases such as "May I be happy, may I be healthy, may I be safe, may I live with ease." Gradually extend these wishes to others, including loved ones, acquaintances, and even those you may have conflicts with. This practice can help foster a sense of connection and reduce feelings of anger and resentment.

7. Mindful Breathing: Mindful breathing is a simple yet effective mindfulness practice. Focus your attention on your breath, observing the natural rhythm of your inhales and exhales. You can count each breath or repeat a

calming word or phrase with each inhale and exhale. This practice can help calm your mind and reduce stress.

8. Mindful Walking: Mindful walking involves paying attention to the sensations of walking, such as the movement of your legs, the contact of your feet with the ground, and the rhythm of your steps. Walk slowly and deliberately, focusing on each step. This practice can be done indoors or outdoors and can help ground you in the present moment.

9. Mindfulness in Daily Activities: You can incorporate mindfulness into everyday activities, such as eating, cleaning, or showering. Focus on the sensory experiences of each activity, such as the taste and texture of food, the feel of water on your skin, or the sounds around you. Practicing mindfulness in daily activities can help you stay present and reduce feelings of overwhelm.

10. Creating a Mindfulness Routine: Consistency is key to benefiting from mindfulness and meditation. Set aside a specific time each day for your practice, whether it's in the morning, during a lunch break, or before bed. Start with just a few minutes each day and gradually increase the duration as you become more comfortable with the practice.

Imagine a man who loses his spouse might find comfort in practicing mindfulness meditation each morning. He begins with a few minutes of mindful breathing, gradually increasing to longer sessions as he becomes more experienced. He also incorporates mindful walking into his daily routine, finding peace and presence in each step.

Integrating mindfulness and meditation into your life can provide a sense of calm, clarity, and emotional balance. These practices offer a way to navigate the intense emotions of grief with greater awareness and compassion. By staying present and accepting your experiences without judgment, you can find a path towards healing and resilience.

Finding Meaning

Finding meaning amid grief can be a transformative part of the healing process. While the pain of loss is inevitable, discovering purpose and significance in your experience can provide comfort, hope, and a renewed sense of direction. Here are some ways to find meaning and purpose while navigating grief:

1. Reflecting on the Relationship: One way to find meaning is to reflect on the relationship you had with the person who passed away. Consider the positive impact they had on your life, the lessons they taught you, and the memories you shared. By focusing on the value and significance of the relationship, you can honour their memory and appreciate the time you had together.

2. Creating a Legacy: Creating a legacy for your loved one can provide a sense of purpose and fulfilment. This might involve starting a scholarship fund, planting a tree, or creating a memorial in their honour. These acts of remembrance can help keep their memory alive and provide a way to continue their influence in the world.

3. Volunteering and Helping Others: Helping others can be a powerful way to find meaning and purpose in the face of loss. Volunteering for a cause that was important

to your loved one or supporting others who are going through similar experiences can provide a sense of connection and fulfilment. It allows you to channel your grief into positive action and make a difference in the lives of others.

4. Engaging in Creative Expression: Creative expression can be a therapeutic way to process grief and find meaning. Writing, painting, music, and other forms of art can help you explore your emotions and tell your story. These creative outlets can provide a sense of release and help you make sense of your grief.

5. Exploring Spirituality: For many individuals, spirituality and religious beliefs play a significant role in finding meaning in grief. Engaging in spiritual practices, such as prayer, meditation, or attending religious services, can provide comfort and a sense of connection to something greater than yourself. Exploring your beliefs and finding solace in your faith can offer a source of strength and hope.

6. Building New Traditions: Creating new traditions and rituals can provide a sense of continuity and purpose. This might involve celebrating your loved one's birthday with a special activity, hosting an annual gathering in their honour, or incorporating their memory into holiday traditions. These rituals can help you feel connected to your loved one and provide a way to honour their legacy.

7. Pursuing Personal Growth: Grief can be an opportunity for personal growth and self-discovery. Reflecting on your own values, goals, and passions can help you find new meaning and purpose. This might involve pursuing new interests, setting new goals, or making positive

changes in your life. Embracing personal growth can help you move forward with a renewed sense of direction.

8. Connecting with Nature: Spending time in nature can provide a sense of peace and perspective. Activities such as hiking, gardening, or simply sitting in a park can help you feel grounded and connected to the natural world. Nature can offer a sense of continuity and remind you of the cycles of life and renewal.

9. Seeking Professional Guidance: Therapy and counselling can provide valuable support for finding meaning in grief. A therapist can help you explore your emotions, identify sources of meaning, and develop coping strategies. Professional guidance can offer new insights and help you navigate the complexities of grief.

10. Practicing Gratitude: Focusing on gratitude can help shift your perspective and find meaning in the midst of loss. Reflecting on the positive aspects of your life, the support you have received, and the memories you cherish can provide a sense of appreciation and hope. Keeping a gratitude journal or sharing moments of gratitude with others can reinforce this practice.

Imagine a woman who loses her son might find meaning by starting a foundation in his name to support children's education. She also engages in creative writing, using her experiences to help others who are grieving. Through these activities, she honours her son's memory and finds a renewed sense of purpose.

Finding meaning in grief is a deeply personal and individual journey. It involves exploring what is important to you, honouring your loved one's legacy, and discovering new sources of purpose and fulfilment. By embracing this journey with openness and compassion, you can transform your grief into a source of strength and hope.

Personal Story - Raj's Resilience

Raj sat on the edge of his bed, staring at the photograph of his wife, Priya. It had been two years since she passed away, but the pain still lingered, a constant reminder of the love they had shared. Priya had been his partner, his confidante, and his best friend. Losing her felt like losing a part of himself, a wound that seemed impossible to heal.

In the immediate aftermath of Priya's death, Raj felt overwhelmed by grief. He struggled to get through each day, the weight of his sorrow making even the simplest tasks feel insurmountable. He withdrew from his friends and family, unable to face their pity and well-meaning but often unhelpful advice. The isolation deepened his despair, creating a cycle of sadness and loneliness.

One evening, as Raj was going through Priya's belongings, he came across a journal she had kept. The pages were filled with her thoughts, dreams, and reflections on their life together. Reading her words brought a sense of comfort and connection, as if she were still with him, guiding him through his grief.

Inspired by Priya's journal, Raj decided to take small steps towards healing. He knew that Priya would want him to find joy and purpose in life, even in her absence. Drawing on the strength of their love, Raj began to explore new ways to cope with his grief.

He started by reconnecting with his friends and family. At first, it was difficult to open up about his feelings, but he soon realized that sharing his pain helped lighten the load. His loved ones offered support, understanding, and practical help, reminding him that he was not alone. These connections provided a lifeline, helping Raj feel less isolated and more supported.

Raj also sought professional help, finding a therapist who specialized in grief counselling. Through therapy, he learned to navigate the complex emotions of grief and develop healthy coping strategies. His therapist introduced him to mindfulness and meditation, practices that helped Raj stay grounded and manage his emotions. These techniques provided a sense of calm and clarity, allowing him to process his grief in a healthier way.

Volunteering became another important aspect of Raj's healing journey. Priya had been passionate about education, and Raj decided to honour her memory by volunteering at a local after-school program. Helping children with their studies and watching them grow and succeed brought Raj a sense of fulfilment and connection. It allowed him to channel his grief into positive action and continue Priya's legacy.

Raj also returned to his love of gardening, a hobby he and Priya had enjoyed together. Tending to the plants and watching them bloom provided a sense of peace and continuity. The garden became a sanctuary, a place where Raj could reflect, remember, and find solace. He planted a tree in Priya's memory, a living tribute to their love and life together.

Creating new traditions helped Raj find meaning and purpose. Each year on Priya's birthday, he organized a community event in her honour, bringing together friends and family to celebrate her life. These gatherings became a source of joy and connection, a way to keep Priya's memory alive and share her spirit with others.

Through these small but significant steps, Raj began to rebuild his life. He learned to live with his grief, understanding that it was a part of him but not all of him. He embraced the support of his loved ones, found fulfilment in volunteering, and reconnected with his passions. Raj's resilience and determination to honour Priya's memory helped him find a new sense of normalcy and joy.

Raj's journey through grief is a testament to the power of love, resilience, and the importance of seeking support. His story illustrates that while the pain of loss may never completely disappear, it is possible to find hope, meaning, and a renewed sense of purpose. By taking small steps towards healing, Raj transformed his grief into a source of strength and continued to live a life filled with love and purpose.

CHAPTER 7: OVERCOMING GRIEF

The Process of Healing

The process of healing from grief is unique for each individual, and it involves navigating through a series of emotional, mental, and physical challenges. Healing does not mean forgetting or erasing the memory of the loved one, but rather finding a way to live with the loss and continuing to move forward with life. Here are some key aspects of the healing process:

1. Acknowledging the Pain: The first step in healing is to acknowledge and accept the pain of loss. Denying or suppressing emotions can prolong the grieving process and make it more difficult to heal. Allowing yourself to feel sadness, anger, guilt, and other emotions is a crucial part of coming to terms with the loss.

2. Allowing Time to Grieve: Healing from grief takes time, and there is no set timeline for when you should feel "better." It is important to give yourself the time and space needed to grieve at your own pace. Some days may be more difficult than others, and that is completely

normal.

3. Seeking Support: Surrounding yourself with supportive friends, family members, or support groups can provide comfort and understanding. Sharing your feelings and experiences with others who understand can help you feel less alone and more validated in your grief.

4. Finding Healthy Outlets: Engaging in activities that provide a sense of relief and expression can be beneficial. This might include physical exercise, creative arts, writing, or other hobbies that allow you to channel your emotions in a positive way.

5. Creating a Routine: Establishing a daily routine can provide a sense of stability and normalcy. Having regular activities and responsibilities can help structure your day and provide a distraction from the intensity of grief.

6. Practicing Self-Compassion: Being kind and gentle with yourself during the healing process is crucial. Recognize that grief is a natural response to loss and that it is okay to have good days and bad days. Treat yourself with the same compassion you would offer to a friend in need.

7. Exploring New Interests: Finding new interests or revisiting old ones can provide a sense of purpose and joy. Engaging in activities that bring you fulfilment can help you focus on the present and future, rather than dwelling solely on the past.

8. Honouring the Memory: Creating rituals or memorials to honour your loved one's memory can provide comfort and a sense of connection. This might involve lighting a

candle, planting a tree, or participating in activities that were meaningful to them.

9. Seeking Professional Help: If the grief feels overwhelming or unmanageable, seeking help from a mental health professional can provide additional support. Therapists and counsellors can offer tools and strategies for coping with grief and help you navigate the healing process.

10. Fostering Resilience: Building resilience involves developing coping skills and finding ways to adapt to the changes brought about by loss. This might include setting new goals, building a support network, and finding meaning and purpose in life despite the grief.

Imagine a man who loses his partner might find healing through a combination of support from friends and family, engaging in his favourite hobby of painting, and seeking therapy to address his intense emotions. He also creates a memorial in his garden to honour his partner's memory, finding comfort in tending to the space they once enjoyed together.

The process of healing from grief is not linear, and there will be ups and downs along the way. It is important to be patient with yourself and recognize that healing is a gradual and ongoing journey. By acknowledging the pain, seeking support, and finding healthy ways to cope, you can navigate the path towards healing and find a renewed sense of hope and purpose.

Building a New Normal

Building a new normal after a significant loss involves adjusting to life without your loved one and finding ways to create a meaningful and fulfilling existence. This process can be challenging, as it requires adapting to changes in routines, roles, and relationships. Here are some strategies for building a new normal:

1. Accepting Change: One of the first steps in building a new normal is accepting that life has changed and will never be the same as it was before the loss. This acceptance does not mean forgetting or moving on from your loved one, but rather finding a way to integrate their memory into your new reality.

2. Redefining Roles: The loss of a loved one can lead to changes in roles and responsibilities. Imagine the death of a spouse might require the surviving partner to take on new roles, such as managing finances or household tasks. It is important to acknowledge these changes and seek support if needed.

3. Establishing New Routines: Creating new routines can provide a sense of stability and structure. This might involve setting regular times for meals, exercise, work, and self-care activities. Establishing new routines can help anchor your day and provide a sense of normalcy.

4. Finding New Interests: Exploring new interests and activities can provide a sense of purpose and fulfilment. This might involve pursuing a hobby you have always been interested in, taking up a new sport, or joining a club or organization. Engaging in new activities can help you focus on the present and future.

5. Maintaining Connections: Staying connected with friends, family, and support groups is crucial for building a new normal. These connections can provide emotional

support, practical help, and a sense of community. It is important to nurture these relationships and seek support when needed.

6. Honouring the Memory: Finding ways to honour your loved one's memory can provide comfort and a sense of connection. This might involve creating a memorial, participating in activities that were meaningful to them, or sharing stories and memories with others. These acts of remembrance can help keep their memory alive and provide a source of solace.

7. Setting Goals: Setting new goals can provide a sense of direction and motivation. These goals can be small, such as completing a daily task, or larger, such as pursuing a new career or education. Setting and achieving goals can help you feel a sense of accomplishment and progress.

8. Practicing Self-Care: Taking care of your physical and emotional well-being is essential for building a new normal. This might involve engaging in regular exercise, eating a balanced diet, getting enough sleep, and practicing mindfulness or relaxation techniques. Prioritizing self-care can help you build resilience and cope with the challenges of grief.

9. Embracing Flexibility: Building a new normal involves being flexible and open to change. There will be ups and downs along the way, and it is important to be patient with yourself. Allow yourself to adapt and adjust as needed, recognizing that the process of rebuilding takes time.

10. Seeking Professional Support: If you find it difficult to build a new normal on your own, seeking help

from a therapist or counsellor can provide additional support. Professional guidance can help you navigate the challenges of grief and develop strategies for creating a meaningful and fulfilling life.

The woman who lost her husband might find it challenging to manage household tasks and finances on her own. She seeks support from family and friends, who offer practical help and emotional support. She also takes up a new hobby, such as gardening, which provides a sense of purpose and fulfilment. By creating new routines, setting goals, and embracing flexibility, she gradually builds a new normal and finds a renewed sense of hope.

Building a new normal after a loss is a gradual and ongoing process. It requires patience, resilience, and the willingness to adapt to changes. By accepting the new reality, finding ways to honour your loved one's memory, and seeking support, you can create a meaningful and fulfilling life despite the grief.

Embracing Change

Embracing change is a crucial part of the grieving process and building a new normal. The loss of a loved one brings significant changes to one's life, and learning to accept and adapt to these changes can lead to growth and healing. Here are some strategies for embracing change during the grieving process:

1. Acknowledging the Reality of Loss: The first step in embracing change is acknowledging the reality of the loss. This involves accepting that life will never be the same and that it is okay to feel a wide range of emotions.

Recognizing the impact of the loss can help you begin to adapt to the new reality.

2. Finding Meaning in Change: Viewing change as an opportunity for growth and personal development can help shift your perspective. Reflecting on the positive aspects of change and finding meaning in your experience can provide a sense of purpose and hope.

3. Setting New Goals: Setting new goals can help you focus on the future and create a sense of direction. These goals can be related to personal growth, career, hobbies, or relationships. Achieving these goals can provide a sense of accomplishment and motivation.

4. Staying Open to New Experiences: Embracing change involves being open to new experiences and opportunities. This might involve trying new activities, meeting new people, or exploring new interests. Staying open to new experiences can help you discover new sources of joy and fulfilment.

5. Seeking Support: Surrounding yourself with supportive friends, family, and community can provide the encouragement and strength needed to embrace change. Sharing your feelings and experiences with others can help you feel understood and supported.

6. Practicing Flexibility: Being flexible and adaptable is important when navigating change. Life may not always go as planned, and it is important to be willing to adjust and make changes as needed. Practicing flexibility can help you cope with the uncertainties and challenges of life after loss.

7. Cultivating Resilience: Building resilience involves

developing coping skills and finding ways to adapt to the changes brought about by loss. This might include practicing mindfulness, seeking professional help, and focusing on self-care. Cultivating resilience can help you navigate change with greater ease and confidence.

8. Honouring the Past While Moving Forward: Embracing change does not mean forgetting

the past. It is important to honour the memory of your loved one while also finding ways to move forward. This might involve creating rituals or traditions that keep their memory alive while also embracing new opportunities and experiences.

9. Finding Joy in Small Moments: Finding joy in small moments can help you embrace change with a positive attitude. This might involve appreciating the beauty of nature, enjoying a favourite activity, or spending time with loved ones. Focusing on moments of joy can provide a sense of balance and hope.

10. Celebrating Progress: Acknowledging and celebrating your progress, no matter how small, can help you stay motivated and positive. Recognizing your achievements and growth can provide a sense of pride and encouragement.

Imagine a man who loses his wife might find it challenging to embrace the changes in his life. He starts by setting small goals, such as cooking a new recipe or taking a daily walk. He seeks support from friends and family, who offer encouragement and companionship. Over time, he becomes more open to new experiences, such as joining a hiking group or taking up a new hobby.

By staying flexible and focusing on moments of joy, he gradually learns to embrace change and finds a renewed sense of purpose.

Embracing change is a dynamic and ongoing process. It requires patience, resilience, and the willingness to adapt to new circumstances. By finding meaning in change, staying open to new experiences, and seeking support, you can navigate the challenges of grief and create a fulfilling life after loss.

Long-term Strategies

Navigating grief is an ongoing journey that often requires long-term strategies to maintain emotional and physical well-being. While the intensity of grief may lessen over time, the impact of loss can continue to influence your life. Here are some long-term strategies to support your ongoing healing and growth:

1. Continuing to Seek Support: Maintaining connections with supportive friends, family, and support groups is essential for long-term well-being. These relationships provide a source of comfort, understanding, and practical help. Regularly reaching out for support can help you navigate ongoing challenges and changes.

2. Engaging in Regular Self-Care: Prioritizing self-care is crucial for long-term health. This includes maintaining a balanced diet, engaging in regular physical activity, getting adequate sleep, and practicing mindfulness or relaxation techniques. Consistent self-care can help you manage stress and maintain emotional balance.

3. Setting and Revisiting Goals: Continuously setting and revisiting goals can provide a sense of direction and

purpose. These goals can evolve over time and reflect your changing interests and circumstances. Achieving goals can boost confidence and provide a sense of accomplishment.

4. Embracing Personal Growth: Grief can be an opportunity for personal growth and self-discovery. Reflecting on your values, goals, and passions can help you find new meaning and purpose. Embracing personal growth can lead to a more fulfilling and resilient life.

5. Creating Lasting Tributes: Finding lasting ways to honour your loved one's memory can provide ongoing comfort and connection. This might involve creating a memorial, establishing a scholarship fund, or participating in activities that were meaningful to them. These tributes can keep their memory alive and provide a sense of continuity.

6. Staying Open to Change: Being open to change and new experiences is important for long-term resilience. Life after loss may bring unexpected opportunities and challenges, and staying flexible can help you adapt and grow. Embracing change can lead to new sources of joy and fulfilment.

7. Practicing Gratitude: Regularly practicing gratitude can help shift your perspective and focus on the positive aspects of your life. Reflecting on the things you are thankful for can provide a sense of appreciation and hope. Keeping a gratitude journal or sharing moments of gratitude with others can reinforce this practice.

8. Engaging in Creative Expression: Continuing to engage in creative activities, such as writing, painting, or music,

can provide an outlet for emotions and a way to process ongoing grief. Creative expression can help you explore your feelings and find new ways to tell your story.

9. Seeking Professional Help When Needed: It is important to recognize when you might need additional support from a mental health professional. Therapy or counselling can provide valuable tools and strategies for managing long-term grief and any new challenges that arise. Professional guidance can help you navigate complex emotions and maintain emotional well-being.

10. Fostering Resilience: Building and maintaining resilience involves developing coping skills and finding ways to adapt to ongoing changes. This might include practicing mindfulness, seeking support, and focusing on self-care. Resilience can help you navigate the ups and downs of life after loss and find strength in the face of adversity.

Imagine a woman who loses her father might find that her grief continues to impact her life long after his death. She engages in regular self-care, sets new goals for her career, and maintains connections with supportive friends and family. She also creates a memorial garden in her father's honour and participates in activities that bring her joy. By staying open to change and seeking professional help when needed, she finds a way to navigate her ongoing grief and build a fulfilling life.

Long-term strategies for coping with grief involve ongoing effort, patience, and resilience. By continuing to seek support, embracing personal growth, and maintaining self-care, you can navigate the ongoing impact of loss and find a path towards healing and fulfilment. Grief is a lifelong journey, but with the right strategies, it is possible to live a meaningful and joyful life.

Personal Story - Fatima's Recovery

Fatima sat on the porch of her family's home, looking out at the garden that her husband, Hassan, had lovingly tended for years. It had been three years since Hassan passed away, but the memory of their life together remained vivid in her mind. Fatima's grief had been overwhelming at first, but through resilience, support, and self-discovery, she had found a path towards recovery.

In the months following Hassan's death, Fatima felt lost and disconnected. The weight of her sorrow made it difficult to engage in daily activities, and she withdrew from her friends and family. The garden, once a place of joy and connection, now felt like a painful reminder of her loss. Fatima struggled to find a sense of purpose and direction.

Recognizing that she needed support, Fatima reached out to her sister, who had always been a source of comfort and understanding. Her sister encouraged her to join a local grief support group, where she could share her feelings with others who understood her pain. Reluctantly, Fatima attended her first meeting and found herself surrounded by compassionate individuals who welcomed her with open arms.

Through the support group, Fatima began to feel less alone in her grief. She listened to the stories of others, finding solace in their shared experiences. The group provided a safe space for her to express her emotions and receive validation and support. Slowly, Fatima started to feel a sense of connection and hope.

Fatima also sought professional help, finding a therapist who specialized in grief counselling. Her therapist introduced her to mindfulness and meditation, practices that helped her stay present and manage her intense emotions. Through therapy, Fatima learned to navigate the complexities of her grief and develop healthy coping strategies.

One day, as Fatima was tending to the garden, she felt a sense of peace and connection to Hassan. She decided to create a memorial garden in his honour, planting his favourite flowers and dedicating a small area to his memory. This project provided a sense of purpose and a way to honour Hassan's legacy. Tending to the garden became a therapeutic and healing activity for Fatima.

Fatima also discovered a passion for painting, an interest she had always wanted to pursue but never found the time for. She enrolled in a local art class and began to explore her creative side. Painting became a way for her to express her emotions and find joy and fulfilment. Her artwork reflected her journey through grief and recovery, capturing the beauty and pain of her experience.

As she continued to heal, Fatima set new goals for herself. She decided to volunteer at a local community centre, where she could support others who were going through difficult times. Helping others provided a sense of purpose and connection, and it allowed Fatima to give back to her community. She found fulfilment in making a difference in the lives of others.

Fatima also maintained connections with her friends and family, who provided ongoing support and encouragement. She communicated her needs openly, allowing her loved ones to understand how to best support her. These relationships became a vital source of strength and comfort.

Creating new traditions helped Fatima keep Hassan's memory alive while also embracing the future. Each year on Hassan's birthday, she organized a family gathering to celebrate his life and share stories and memories. These gatherings became a source of joy and connection, allowing Fatima to honour Hassan's legacy in a meaningful way.

Through these small but significant steps, Fatima found a path towards recovery. She learned to live with her grief, understanding that it was a part of her but not all of her. She embraced the support of her loved ones, found fulfilment in volunteering and creative expression, and created new traditions that honoured Hassan's memory.

Fatima's recovery is a testament to the power of resilience, support, and self-discovery. Her journey illustrates that while the pain of loss may never completely disappear, it is possible to find hope, meaning, and a renewed sense of purpose. By taking small steps towards healing and embracing new opportunities, Fatima transformed her grief into a source of strength and continued to live a life filled with love and fulfilment.

CHAPTER 8: GRIEVING THE LOSS OF A CHILD

Unique Aspects of Losing a Child

Grieving the loss of a child is one of the most profound and heart-wrenching experiences one can endure. The pain is often described as unparalleled, a void that seems impossible to fill. The unique aspects of this type of grief set it apart from other losses, creating an intricate web of emotions that can be incredibly challenging to navigate.

The death of a child shatters the natural order of life. Parents expect to see their children grow, flourish, and outlive them. When this expectation is abruptly cut short, it feels like an unnatural and devastating blow. The future that was imagined, filled with milestones, dreams, and shared experiences, is irrevocably altered. This disruption of the expected life course intensifies the grief, as it is not only the loss of the child but also the loss of their future.

One of the unique aspects of losing a child is the intensity of the bond between parent and child. This bond, forged from the moment of conception or adoption, is deeply rooted in a sense of responsibility, love, and protection. When a child dies, parents may feel an overwhelming sense of guilt and helplessness, questioning what they could have done differently to prevent the loss. This self-blame can be a significant barrier to healing, making it crucial to address these feelings with compassion and understanding.

The loss of a child also affects the entire family dynamic. Siblings, grandparents, and extended family members all experience the grief in their own ways, creating a ripple effect that can strain relationships and communication. Siblings may feel neglected as parents focus on their own grief, or they may struggle with their own feelings of loss and guilt. It is important to recognize and address these complex family dynamics, ensuring that all members receive the support they need.

Cultural and societal expectations around grieving can further complicate the experience. Parents may feel pressure to "move on" or to be strong for their surviving children, suppressing their own emotions in the process. This societal pressure can lead to feelings of isolation and misunderstanding. Creating a supportive environment where parents can express their grief openly and without judgment is essential for healing.

One of the most heart-wrenching aspects of losing a child is the pervasive sense of lost potential. Parents mourn not only the child they knew but also the person they would have become. The birthdays, graduations, weddings, and other milestones that will never be celebrated are a constant reminder of the loss. This sense of lost potential can make it difficult to find closure, as the grieving process extends far into the future.

The grieving process for parents who have lost a child is often long and complex. It is not uncommon for parents to experience intense grief for many years, with periods of acute sorrow triggered by anniversaries, holidays, and other significant dates. The pain may ebb and flow, but the absence of the child is a constant presence in their lives. Understanding that this prolonged grief is normal and valid is crucial for both parents and those supporting them.

In the face of such an overwhelming loss, finding ways to honour and remember the child can provide a source of comfort and connection. Creating a memorial, establishing a scholarship fund, or participating in charitable activities in the child's name can help keep their memory alive and provide a sense of purpose. These acts of remembrance can be healing, allowing parents to channel their grief into positive action.

A couple who unfortunately lost their young daughter might find solace in creating a garden in her memory. Planting flowers and trees that bloom each year serves as a living tribute to her life, a place where they can reflect and remember. They might also start a community event in her honour, bringing people together to celebrate her spirit and keep her memory alive.

Grieving the loss of a child is an arduous journey that requires immense strength, resilience, and support. It is a unique and deeply personal experience, filled with intense emotions and complex dynamics. By acknowledging the unique aspects of this grief, offering compassionate support, and finding meaningful ways to remember the child, parents can navigate this difficult path and find moments of healing and hope.

Parental Grief

Parental grief is an all-encompassing, profound sorrow that can feel like an unending storm. The loss of a child leaves parents grappling with a myriad of intense emotions, from overwhelming sadness to profound guilt and anger. Each parent's journey through grief is unique, but the shared experience of losing a child binds them in a way that words often fail to capture.

The bond between a parent and child is unparalleled. It is built on love, protection, and dreams for the future. When a child dies, this bond is cruelly severed, leaving parents with a deep sense of emptiness. The future they envisioned, filled with their child's milestones and achievements, is suddenly gone. This loss of potential and shattered dreams makes parental grief particularly devastating.

One of the most challenging aspects of parental grief is the pervasive sense of guilt. Parents may find themselves trapped in a cycle of "what if" and "if only" thinking, questioning every decision and action leading up to their child's death. This self-blame can be paralyzing, preventing parents from moving forward in their grieving process. Parents must recognize that these feelings, while natural, are often unfounded. Seeking professional support to work through these emotions can be incredibly beneficial.

Anger is another common emotion in parental grief. This anger can be directed at various targets, including oneself, medical professionals, or even the child for leaving them. It can also be a response to the perceived unfairness of the loss. Anger is a natural part of the grieving process, but it is important to find healthy ways to express and manage it. Physical activity, creative expression, and therapy can provide outlets for this intense emotion.

The grief of losing a child can also strain marital and familial relationships. Parents may grieve differently, leading to misunderstandings and conflict. One parent might feel the need to talk about their child constantly, while the other may prefer to grieve in silence. Recognizing and respecting each other's grieving styles is crucial for maintaining a supportive relationship. Couples counselling can help navigate these differences and foster open communication.

Siblings are also profoundly affected by the loss of a child. They may experience their own grief while also feeling the weight of their parents' sorrow. It is important to provide support and validation for their feelings, ensuring that they do not feel neglected or overlooked. Family therapy can help address the complex dynamics that arise from such a significant loss and ensure that all family members receive the support they need.

Amid intense grief, parents may find it difficult to perform everyday tasks and responsibilities. The weight of their sorrow can make it challenging to focus on work, maintain household chores, or care for other children. It is important to prioritize self-care and seek help when needed. Friends, family, and community resources can provide practical support, allowing parents the space to grieve and heal.

Creating rituals and memorials to honour the child's memory can provide a sense of comfort and connection. This might involve lighting a candle, creating a scrapbook, or participating in activities that the child loved. These acts of remembrance can keep the child's memory alive and provide a source of solace. Imagine a mother who loses her son might find comfort in writing letters to him, expressing her thoughts and feelings. She might also create a memory box filled with his favourite toys, drawings, and mementos.

Support groups for bereaved parents can offer a valuable sense of community and understanding. Sharing experiences with others who have faced similar losses can provide validation and reduce feelings of isolation. These groups can also offer practical advice and coping strategies, helping parents navigate their grief. Think about a father who loses his daughter might find solace in a support group for grieving fathers, where he can share his story and connect with others who understand his pain.

Seeking professional support from therapists or grief counsellors can provide additional tools and strategies for coping with parental grief. Therapy can offer a safe space to explore complex emotions, address feelings of guilt and anger, and develop healthy coping mechanisms. Imagine a couple who loses their child might attend couples therapy to strengthen their relationship and find ways to support each other through their grief.

The journey of parental grief is long and arduous, but with compassionate support and understanding, parents can find moments of healing and hope. By acknowledging the depth of their loss, seeking help, and finding meaningful ways to remember their child, parents can navigate the difficult path of grief and begin to rebuild their lives.

Sibling Grief

Sibling grief is a unique and often overlooked aspect of the grieving process. The bond between siblings is complex and deeply rooted in shared experiences, memories, and a lifetime of interactions. When a sibling dies, the surviving siblings face a profound loss that affects their sense of identity, family dynamics, and future. Understanding and addressing sibling grief is essential for providing comprehensive support to the entire family.

The relationship between siblings is unlike any other. Siblings are often each other's first friends, confidantes, and rivals. They share a common history and a deep connection that shapes their identity. When a sibling dies, this connection is abruptly severed, leaving the surviving siblings with a sense of emptiness and disorientation. The loss of a sibling can feel like losing a part of oneself, as well as the shared future they envisioned together.

One of the unique challenges of sibling grief is the sense of being overshadowed by the parents' grief. Surviving siblings may feel that their own grief is not as significant or valid compared to the immense sorrow of their parents. They might also feel the need to be strong for their parents, suppressing their own emotions in an attempt to provide support. It is crucial to recognize and validate the grief of siblings, ensuring that they have the space and support to express their emotions.

Guilt is a common emotion in sibling grief. Surviving siblings may feel guilty for being alive while their brother or sister is not. They might also feel regret for past conflicts or missed opportunities to connect. This guilt can be compounded by a sense of responsibility, wondering if they could have done something to prevent the loss. Addressing these feelings of guilt through open communication and professional support can help siblings navigate their grief.

The loss of a sibling can also disrupt the family dynamic. Siblings may struggle with changes in roles and responsibilities, as well as the emotional distance that can arise from differing grieving styles. Imagine one sibling might seek solace in talking about the deceased, while another might prefer to grieve privately. Respecting and understanding these differences is essential for maintaining a supportive family environment.

Sibling grief can manifest in various ways, including behavioural changes, withdrawal from social activities, academic struggles, and physical symptoms. It is important to be aware of these signs and provide appropriate support. Schools, counsellors, and community resources can play a vital role in helping siblings cope with their grief. Think about a school counsellor might offer individual or group sessions to support grieving students and provide a safe space to express their feelings.

Maintaining routines and traditions can provide a sense of stability and normalcy for grieving siblings. Engaging in activities that the deceased sibling enjoyed or creating new traditions in their honour can help keep their memory alive. Imagine a family might celebrate the deceased sibling's birthday each year with a special meal or a day of activities they loved. These rituals can provide comfort and a sense of connection.

Encouraging open communication within the family is crucial for supporting sibling grief. Creating a safe space where all family members can share their feelings, memories, and concerns can foster understanding and healing. Family meetings or informal gatherings can provide opportunities for these conversations. Imagine a family might set aside time each week to check in with each other, share stories about the deceased sibling, and discuss their emotions.

Support groups specifically for grieving siblings can offer a valuable sense of community and understanding. These groups provide a space for siblings to connect with others who have experienced similar losses, shared their stories, and received validation and support. Think about a teenager who loses her brother might find comfort in a support group for grieving teens, where she can talk openly about her feelings and connect with peers who understand her pain.

Seeking professional support, such as therapy or counselling, can provide additional tools and strategies for coping with sibling grief. Therapists can help siblings explore their emotions, address feelings of guilt and anger, and develop healthy coping mechanisms. Imagine a young boy who loses his sister might benefit from play therapy, where he can express his emotions through creative activities and games.

Sibling grief is a complex and deeply personal experience that requires compassionate support and understanding. By acknowledging the unique aspects of sibling grief, providing appropriate resources, and fostering open communication, families can navigate this difficult journey together. Siblings can find ways to honour their lost brother or sister, maintain their connection, and move forward with resilience and hope.

Coping Strategies

Coping with the loss of a child requires a multifaceted approach that addresses the emotional, physical, and social aspects of grief. While there is no one-size-fits-all solution, various coping strategies can help parents and siblings navigate this profound loss and find a path towards healing. Here are some effective coping strategies for grieving the loss of a child:

1. Allowing Yourself to Grieve: It is essential to allow yourself to grieve fully. This means allowing yourself to feel a wide range of emotions, including sadness, anger, guilt, and despair. Grieving is a natural response to loss, and it is important to honour your emotions without judgment.

2. Seeking Professional Support: Therapy or counselling can provide a safe space to explore your emotions and develop healthy coping strategies. Grief counsellors are trained to help individuals navigate the complexities of loss and can offer valuable tools for managing intense emotions.

3. Joining Support Groups: Connecting with others who have experienced similar losses can provide a sense of

community and understanding. Support groups offer a space to share your story, receive validation, and learn from others' experiences. These groups can be found through local community centres, hospitals, and online platforms.

4. Practicing Self-Care: Taking care of your physical and emotional well-being is crucial during the grieving process. This includes maintaining a balanced diet, engaging in regular physical activity, getting adequate sleep, and practicing relaxation techniques. Prioritizing self-care can help you manage stress and maintain emotional balance.

5. Engaging in Creative Expression: Creative activities such as writing, painting, music, or crafting can provide an outlet for your emotions and a way to process your grief. These activities allow you to express your feelings in a non-verbal way and can be therapeutic and healing.

6. Establishing New Routines: Creating new routines can provide a sense of stability and normalcy. Having regular activities and responsibilities can help structure your day and provide a distraction from the intensity of grief. This might include setting regular times for meals, exercise, work, and self-care activities.

7. Honouring the Memory: Finding meaningful ways to remember and honour your child can provide comfort and a sense of connection. This might involve creating a memorial, planting a tree, or participating in activities that were meaningful to them. These acts of remembrance can keep their memory alive and provide a source of solace.

8. Fostering Open Communication: Encouraging open communication within the family can help everyone express their feelings and support each other. Creating a safe space where all family members can share their emotions, memories, and concerns can foster understanding and healing.

9. Exploring Spirituality: For many individuals, spirituality and religious beliefs play a significant role in coping with grief. Engaging in spiritual practices, such as prayer, meditation, or attending religious services, can provide comfort and a sense of connection to something greater than yourself.

10. Finding Joy in Small Moments: Finding joy in small moments can help you embrace change with a positive attitude. This might involve appreciating the beauty of nature, enjoying a favourite activity, or spending time with loved ones. Focusing on moments of joy can provide a sense of balance and hope.

11. Practicing Mindfulness and Meditation: Mindfulness and meditation can help you stay present and manage the overwhelming emotions of grief. These practices encourage acceptance and compassion towards yourself, allowing you to navigate the complexities of loss with greater ease.

12. Building Resilience: Developing resilience involves finding ways to adapt to the changes brought about by loss. This might include setting new goals, building a support network, and focusing on self-care. Resilience can help you navigate the ups and downs of life after loss and find strength in the face of adversity.

The couple who lost their young daughter might find comfort in creating a memorial garden in her honour. They seek therapy to address their intense emotions and join a support group for grieving parents, where they connect with others who understand their pain. They also practice mindfulness meditation daily, which helps them stay grounded and manage their grief.

Coping with the loss of a child is a deeply personal and challenging journey that requires compassion, resilience, and support. By incorporating these coping strategies and seeking help when needed, parents and siblings can navigate their grief and find moments of healing and hope.

Personal Story - Olivia's Loss

Olivia stood in her daughter's bedroom, the soft pink walls and carefully arranged toys a stark contrast to the emptiness she felt inside. It had been a year since her daughter, Lily, passed away, but the pain was as sharp and relentless as it had been on that dreadful day. Olivia's grief was a constant companion, an ever-present shadow that coloured every moment of her life.

In the immediate aftermath of Lily's death, Olivia felt as though she were moving through a haze. Each day was a struggle to get out of bed, to face the world without her vibrant, joyful little girl. The routines that had once brought structure and comfort now felt hollow and meaningless. Olivia withdrew from friends and family, unable to bear their pity or well-meaning but empty reassurances.

Recognizing that she needed help, Olivia reached out

to a therapist who specialized in grief counselling. In the safe, supportive space of her therapist's office, Olivia began to explore the depths of her sorrow. Her therapist introduced her to mindfulness and meditation, practices that helped Olivia stay present and manage her overwhelming emotions. Through therapy, Olivia learned to navigate the complexities of her grief and develop healthy coping strategies.

One of the first steps in Olivia's healing journey was allowing herself to grieve fully. She permitted herself to feel the full spectrum of her emotions, from deep sadness to anger and guilt. She understood that these feelings were a natural response to her loss and that honouring them was a crucial part of her healing process.

Olivia also found solace in joining a support group for parents who had lost children. The group provided a space where she could share her story and connect with others who understood her pain. Listening to the experiences of other parents, and sharing her own, helped Olivia feel less alone. The support group became a lifeline, offering validation and understanding that she couldn't find elsewhere.

To honour Lily's memory, Olivia decided to create a memorial garden in their backyard. She planted Lily's favourite flowers and added a small bench where she could sit and reflect. Tending to the garden became a therapeutic and healing activity for Olivia. Each bloom was a reminder of her daughter's life and the love they shared.

Engaging in creative expression also played a significant role in Olivia's healing. She began to paint, using colours and shapes to express her emotions. Her artwork became a way to process her grief and find a sense of release. Olivia's paintings, filled with vibrant hues and intricate patterns, reflected her journey through sorrow and healing.

On her journey of healing Olivia set new goals for herself. She decided to volunteer at a local children's hospital, where she could offer support to other families facing difficult times. Helping others provided a sense of purpose and connection, allowing Olivia to channel her grief into positive action. She found fulfilment in making a difference in the lives of others, and it gave her a renewed sense of hope.

Creating new traditions helped Olivia keep Lily's memory alive while also embracing the future. Each year on Lily's birthday, Olivia organized a family gathering to celebrate her life and share stories and memories. These gatherings became a source of joy and connection, allowing Olivia to honour Lily's legacy in a meaningful way.

Maintaining connections with friends and family was also crucial for Olivia's recovery. She communicated her needs openly, allowing her loved ones to understand how to best support her. These relationships provided ongoing support and encouragement, helping Olivia navigate the ups and downs of her grief.

Through these baby steps but significant, Olivia found a path towards healing. She learned to live with her grief, understanding that it was a part of her but not all of her. She embraced the support of her loved ones, found fulfilment in volunteering and creative expression, and created new traditions that honoured Lily's memory.

Olivia's journey through grief is a testament to the power of resilience, support, and self-discovery. Her story illustrates that while the pain of loss may never completely disappear, it is possible to find hope, meaning, and a renewed sense of purpose. By taking small steps towards healing and embracing new opportunities, Olivia transformed her grief into a source of strength and continued to live a life filled with love and fulfilment.

CHAPTER 9: GRIEVING THE LOSS OF A SPOUSE

The Void Left Behind

The loss of a spouse leaves an indescribable void, a profound absence that permeates every aspect of life. This person was not just a partner but often a best friend, confidante, and co-navigator through life's journey. The void left behind is more than physical; it is emotional, spiritual, and deeply personal.

The daily routines and shared experiences that once brought joy and stability now serve as constant reminders of the loss. Simple activities such as making coffee in the morning, watching a favourite TV show, or even sitting in silence are now imbued with a sense of emptiness. The home, once filled with shared memories and mutual comfort, can feel like an echo chamber of grief.

One of the most challenging aspects of losing a spouse is the disruption of the intimate partnership. This partnership, built on mutual support, love, and shared responsibilities, is suddenly severed, leaving the surviving spouse to navigate life alone. This can be particularly difficult when the partnership involved a division of roles and responsibilities that now must be restructured.

The emotional impact of this void can be overwhelming. Grief can manifest as deep sadness, loneliness, anger, and even guilt. These emotions can fluctuate wildly, leaving the surviving spouse feeling as though they are on an emotional rollercoaster. It is important to acknowledge and validate these feelings, understanding that they are a natural response to such a profound loss.

Support from friends, family, and community can provide much-needed comfort during this time. However, it is not uncommon for the surviving spouse to feel isolated even in the presence of others. The unique bond shared with a spouse is irreplaceable, and well-meaning support from others can sometimes feel insufficient or superficial. Finding a balance between seeking support and allowing oneself to grieve privately is crucial.

An elderly man who lost his wife might struggle with the silence and stillness of his home. He finds solace in talking to their children and grandchildren, who share fond memories and stories of their time together. These conversations help him feel connected to his wife and provide a sense of continuity.

Maintaining a sense of routine can also help navigate the void left behind. Establishing new routines or adjusting existing ones can provide a sense of structure and normalcy. Engaging in activities that bring comfort and joy, whether they are new hobbies or cherished pastimes, can help fill some of the emptiness.

Creating a memorial or tribute to the spouse can provide a tangible way to honour their memory. This might involve setting up a small shrine with photographs and mementos, planting a tree in their name, or participating in a charity event that was important to them. These acts of remembrance can help keep their memory alive and provide a sense of purpose.

Think about a woman who loses her husband might create a scrapbook filled with photographs, letters, and memories of their life together. She spends time each week adding to the scrapbook, finding solace in this creative expression of her love and grief.

Seeking professional support from a therapist or grief counsellor can offer additional tools and strategies for coping with the void left behind. Therapy can provide a safe space to explore complex emotions, develop healthy coping mechanisms, and find ways to move forward. Support groups for widows and widowers can also offer a sense of community and understanding.

Navigating the void left behind after the loss of a spouse is an ongoing journey. It requires patience, resilience, and the willingness to embrace both the pain and the possibility of healing. By acknowledging the depth of the loss, seeking support, and finding meaningful ways to remember the spouse, individuals can begin to navigate this difficult path and find moments of peace and hope.

Redefining Identity

The loss of a spouse not only leaves a profound

emotional void but also necessitates a redefinition of identity. Spouses often share intertwined identities, with each partner's sense of self deeply connected to their relationship. When one partner dies, the surviving spouse must navigate the challenging process of rediscovering who they are as an individual.

This redefinition of identity can be daunting. The roles and responsibilities once shared now fall solely on the surviving spouse, requiring adjustments in daily life and personal identity. Tasks and decisions that were once collaborative now must be faced alone, which can be overwhelming and disorienting.

One of the first steps in redefining identity is to acknowledge the depth of the loss and its impact on one's sense of self. It is important to recognize that grief and confusion are natural responses to such a significant change. Allowing oneself to mourn not just the loss of the spouse but also the loss of the shared identity is a crucial part of the healing process.

Laxmi, who lost her husband recently struggles with the sudden absence of his presence and the roles he played in their life together. She finds it challenging to manage household finances and make important decisions on her own. Acknowledging these challenges and seeking support from friends, family, or professionals can help her navigate this difficult transition.

Engaging in self-reflection can be a valuable tool in redefining identity. Taking time to explore personal values, interests, and goals can help the surviving spouse reconnect with themselves. Journaling, meditating, or simply spending time in contemplation can provide insights into who they are and who they want to become.

Rediscovering and pursuing personal interests can also aid in the redefinition of identity. Engaging in hobbies, activities, or passions that may have been set aside during the marriage can provide a sense of fulfilment and purpose. Think about a man who loses his wife might reignite his passion for painting, finding solace and self-expression in his art.

Creating new routines and establishing a sense of independence can help build a new sense of identity. This might involve setting new goals, developing new skills, or exploring new opportunities. Taking small steps towards independence can build confidence and resilience, helping the surviving spouse navigate their new reality.

Support from friends, family, and community can provide a crucial foundation during this process. Sharing experiences and seeking advice from those who have gone through similar losses can offer valuable perspectives and encouragement. Support groups for widows and widowers can provide a sense of community and understanding, helping individuals feel less alone in their journey.

Consider, Imagine a woman who lost her husband might join a support group for widows. Through the group, she connects with others who understand her pain and shares her experiences of redefining her identity. These connections provide validation and support, helping her feel more confident in her ability to move forward.

Professional support from therapists or life coaches can also offer guidance in navigating the redefinition of identity. These professionals can help individuals explore their emotions, set goals, and develop strategies for personal growth. Therapy can provide a safe space to process complex feelings and build a new sense of self.

Embracing change and being open to new experiences is an important part of redefining identity. While it can be difficult to let go of the past, finding ways to integrate the memory of the spouse into the new identity can provide a sense of continuity and connection. This might involve creating rituals, participating in activities that honour the spouse's memory, or finding ways to keep their legacy alive.

Think about the person who lost his wife might start a scholarship fund in her name, supporting students in a field she was passionate about. This act of service provides a sense of purpose and connection, helping him integrate her memory into his new identity.

Redefining identity after the loss of a spouse is a gradual and ongoing process. It requires patience, self-compassion, and the willingness to embrace both the pain of the loss and the growth potential. By exploring personal values and interests, seeking support, and being open to new experiences, individuals can navigate this journey and find a renewed sense of self and purpose.

The Role of Memories

Memories play a pivotal role in the grieving process, serving as both a source of comfort and a catalyst for sorrow. When a spouse dies, the memories of the time spent together become cherished treasures, yet they can also evoke a deep sense of loss. Navigating the complex role of memories is a crucial aspect of coping with grief and finding a way to move forward.

One of the most challenging aspects of grief is the constant presence of memories. These can be triggered by seemingly mundane events—a favourite song on the radio, a particular scent, or a familiar place. While these memories can bring comfort, they can also intensify feelings of longing and sadness. It is important to acknowledge these emotions and allow oneself to experience them fully.

Creating intentional spaces and times to remember the spouse can help manage the emotional impact of these memories. This might involve setting aside a specific time each day or week to reflect on memories, looking through photo albums, or writing down favourite moments. By creating structured times for remembrance, individuals can honour their spouse's memory while also maintaining control over when and how they engage with these memories.

Imagine a woman who loses her husband might dedicate Sunday afternoons to looking through their wedding album and reminiscing about their life together. This ritual provides a safe and intentional space for her to connect with her memories and emotions.

Memorializing the spouse through creative expression can also be a powerful way to honour their memory. Writing, painting, music, or crafting can provide an outlet for emotions and a way to keep the spouse's memory alive. These creative activities can be therapeutic, allowing individuals to process their grief in a tangible and meaningful way.

Think about he might want to write a series of letters to her, expressing his thoughts and feelings. These letters become a cherished collection, a testament to their love and his journey through grief.

Incorporating memories into daily life can provide a sense of continuity and connection. This might involve small acts such as wearing a piece of jewellery that belonged to the spouse, cooking their favourite meal, or maintaining traditions that were important to them. These acts of remembrance can help integrate the memory of the spouse into the new reality, providing comfort and a sense of presence.

Sharing memories with others can also be a healing experience. Talking about the spouse with friends, family, or support groups can provide validation and connection. These conversations can reinforce the bond with the spouse and keep their memory alive in the hearts of those who loved them.

Imagine a woman who loses her husband might find solace in sharing stories about him with their children and grandchildren. These shared memories create a sense of continuity and help preserve his legacy within the family.

Creating a physical memorial can provide a tangible way to honour the spouse's memory. This might involve setting up a small shrine with photographs and mementoes, planting a tree in their name, or participating in a charity event that was important to them. These physical acts of remembrance can provide a focal point for grief and a way to celebrate the spouse's life.

Again, Think about the unfortunate couple who lost their son and might plant a tree in their backyard in his memory. Each year, they gather around the tree to celebrate his birthday, sharing stories and memories as they watch the tree grow.

Seeking professional support can help individuals navigate the complex emotions associated with memories. Therapists and grief counsellors can provide tools and strategies for managing the emotional impact of memories and finding ways to honour the spouse's memory. Support groups can also offer a space to share memories and connect with others who understand the pain of loss.

Memories are an integral part of the grieving process, providing both comfort and sorrow. By creating intentional spaces for remembrance, engaging in creative expression, and incorporating memories into daily life, individuals can honour their spouse's memory and find a way to move forward. The role of memories in grief is multifaceted, but with support and intentionality, they can become a source of strength and healing.

Personal Story - Martin's Journey

Martin sat on the edge of his bed, the silence of his empty home pressing in around him. It had been six months since his wife, Eleanor, passed away, and the weight of his grief was a constant companion. Their home, once filled with laughter and love, now felt like a hollow shell. Martin's journey through grief was marked by deep sorrow, but also by moments of connection, remembrance, and resilience.

In the early days after Eleanor's death, Martin struggled to find his footing. Each day felt like an insurmountable challenge, the routines they had shared now painful reminders of her absence. Making coffee in the morning, watching their favourite shows, even walking through the rooms of their home—all were tinged with a profound sense of loss. Martin felt adrift, his identity as Eleanor's husband now a painful memory.

Recognizing the need for support, Martin reached out to a grief counsellor. In the safe space of his counsellor's office, Martin began to explore the depths of his sorrow. His counsellor introduced him to mindfulness and meditation, practices that helped him stay present and manage his overwhelming emotions. Through therapy, Martin learned to navigate the complexities of his grief and develop healthy coping strategies.

One of the most significant steps in Martin's healing journey was creating intentional spaces for remembrance. He set aside time each evening to sit quietly with Eleanor's memory. He would light a candle, look through their photo albums, and reflect on the life they had built together. This ritual provided a structured time for Martin to connect with his emotions and honour Eleanor's memory.

Martin also found solace in creative expression. He had always enjoyed writing, and he began to pen letters to Eleanor, expressing his thoughts and feelings. These letters became a cherished collection, a testament to their love and his journey through grief. Writing allowed Martin to process his emotions in a tangible and meaningful way.

To honour Eleanor's memory, Martin decided to create a garden in their backyard. Eleanor had loved gardening, and this project felt like a fitting tribute. He planted her favourite flowers and added a bench where he could sit and reflect. Tending to the garden became a therapeutic and healing activity for Martin. Each bloom was a reminder of Eleanor's life and the love they shared.

Martin also sought connection with others who understood his pain. He joined a support group for widowers, where he found a community of men who had experienced similar losses. The group provided a space for Martin to share his story and connect with others who validated his grief. These connections offered comfort and understanding, helping Martin feel less alone in his journey.

As he continued to heal, Martin set new goals for himself. He decided to volunteer at a local community centre, where he could support others who were facing difficult times. Helping others provided a sense of purpose and fulfilment, allowing Martin to channel his grief into positive action. He found joy in making a difference in the lives of others, and it gave him a renewed sense of hope.

Creating new traditions helped Martin keep Eleanor's memory alive while also embracing the future. Each year on Eleanor's birthday, he organized a family gathering to celebrate her life and share stories and memories. These gatherings became a source of joy and connection, allowing Martin to honour Eleanor's legacy in a meaningful way.

Maintaining connections with friends and family was also crucial for Martin's recovery. He communicated his needs openly, allowing his loved ones to understand how to best support him. These relationships provided ongoing support and encouragement, helping Martin navigate the ups and downs of his grief.

Through these small but significant steps, Martin found a path towards healing. He learned to live with his grief, understanding that it was a part of him but not all of him. He embraced the support of his loved ones, found fulfilment in volunteering and creative expression, and created new traditions that honoured Eleanor's memory.

Martin's journey through grief is a testament to the power of resilience, support, and self-discovery. His story illustrates that while the pain of loss may never completely disappear, it is possible to find hope, meaning, and a renewed sense of purpose. By taking small steps towards healing and embracing new opportunities, Martin transformed his grief into a source of strength and continued to live a life filled with love and fulfilment.

CHAPTER 10: GRIEVING THE LOSS OF A PARENT

The Foundation of Our Lives

Losing a parent is a profound and deeply personal experience. Parents are often the foundation of our lives, the pillars of support and guidance that shape our identity and values. When a parent dies, the loss reverberates through every aspect of our existence, leaving a void that can feel insurmountable.

Parents are our first caregivers, teachers, and role models. They nurture us, guide us, and provide a sense of security and belonging. The bond between a parent and child is unique and multifaceted, encompassing unconditional love, shared experiences, and a lifetime of memories. When a parent dies, it can feel as though the very ground beneath us has shifted.

One of the most challenging aspects of losing a parent is the loss of their wisdom and guidance. Parents often serve as a source of advice and support throughout our lives. Their absence can leave us feeling adrift, uncertain of how to navigate life's challenges without their steady presence. It is important to acknowledge this sense of loss and seek out new sources of support and guidance.

A young girl who lost her father struggles with the absence of his advice and encouragement. She seeks support from her mother and siblings, who share their own experiences and insights. Together, they create a new network of support that helps them navigate their grief and move forward.

The loss of a parent can also bring up unresolved issues and complex emotions. Relationships with parents are often layered with both love and conflict, and their death can leave us grappling with feelings of regret, guilt, and unfinished business. It is important to address these emotions and find ways to process and heal from them.

Engaging in self-reflection and seeking professional support can be valuable tools in navigating these complex emotions. Therapy can provide a safe space to explore unresolved issues, work through feelings of guilt and regret, and develop healthy coping strategies. Think about a man who loses his mother might seek therapy to address lingering feelings of resentment and guilt, finding a way to heal and move forward.

Honouring the memory of a parent is a crucial part of the grieving process. Creating rituals and memorials that celebrate their life and legacy can provide comfort and a sense of connection. This might involve setting up a small shrine with photographs and mementoes, writing letters to them, or participating in activities that were meaningful to them.

The woman who lost her mother might create a memory

box filled with her mother's favourite jewellery, letters, and photographs. Each year on her mother's birthday, she takes time to reflect on their memories and share stories with her family. This ritual provides a sense of continuity and helps keep her mother's memory alive.

Maintaining connections with family and friends can provide much-needed support during this difficult time. Sharing memories and stories with loved ones can help keep the parent's legacy alive and provide a sense of comfort and belonging. Support groups for those who have lost parents can also offer a space to connect with others who understand the unique challenges of this type of grief.

A man who loses his father might find solace in joining a support group for adults who have lost parents. Through the group, he connects with others who share their experiences and offer support. These connections provide validation and understanding, helping him feel less alone in his grief.

Finding ways to integrate the memory of the parent into daily life can provide a sense of comfort and connection. This might involve continuing traditions that were important to them, wearing a piece of their jewellery, or cooking their favourite recipes. These acts of remembrance can help keep the parent's presence alive and provide a source of solace.

A woman who loses her father might continue their tradition of Sunday morning walks. Each week, she takes a walk in the park they used to visit together, reflecting on their conversations and the wisdom he shared. This ritual helps her feel connected to him and provides a sense of peace.

Losing a parent is a deeply transformative experience that requires compassion, resilience, and support. By acknowledging the depth of the loss, seeking out new sources of guidance, and finding meaningful ways to honour their memory, individuals can navigate this difficult journey and find moments of healing and hope. The foundation that parents provide remains a part of us, shaping who we are and guiding us as we move forward.

The Intergenerational Impact

The loss of a parent often has a profound intergenerational impact, affecting not only the immediate family but also future generations. This ripple effect can influence how grief is processed and experienced within the family, shaping the dynamics and emotional health of each member. Understanding and addressing this intergenerational impact is crucial for fostering a supportive and healing environment.

When a parent dies, the surviving family members must navigate their grief while also managing the changes in family roles and responsibilities. This shift can be particularly challenging for adult children who may find themselves assuming new caregiving roles for surviving parents or younger siblings. The burden of these new responsibilities can add to the emotional strain, making it essential to seek support and open lines of communication within the family.

Imagine after the death of their mother, two sisters find themselves responsible for caring for their elderly father. The increased responsibilities strain their relationship, leading to conflict and misunderstandings. By seeking family counselling, they are able to communicate more effectively and share the caregiving duties, finding a new balance that honours their mother's memory while supporting each other.

The loss of a grandparent can also deeply affect grandchildren, who may experience their own unique form of grief. The bond between grandparents and grandchildren is often characterized by unconditional love and a sense of continuity. The death of a grandparent can disrupt this connection, leading to feelings of loss and confusion. It is important to include grandchildren in the grieving process, providing them with support and opportunities to express their emotions.

Think about a young boy who loses his grandmother might feel isolated in his grief. His parents encourage him to create a memory scrapbook filled with photographs, drawings, and stories about his grandmother. This activity helps him process his emotions and keeps his grandmother's memory alive.

Family traditions and rituals can provide a sense of continuity and connection, helping to honour the memory of the deceased parent. These traditions can be adapted to include all family members, fostering a sense of unity and shared remembrance. Imagine a family might continue to celebrate holidays in the same way their parent did, incorporating their favourite dishes, decorations, and activities.

Intergenerational impact also extends to the way grief is modelled and expressed within the family. Children and grandchildren often look to the older generations for cues on how to navigate their own grief. Demonstrating healthy coping mechanisms, such as open communication, emotional expression, and seeking support, can provide a positive example for younger family members.

Imagine a father who loses his own parent might openly share his grief with his children, allowing them to see his vulnerability and resilience. He encourages them to talk about their feelings and provides support as they navigate their own grief. This openness fosters a supportive family environment where emotions are validated and addressed.

Cultural and societal expectations can also influence the intergenerational impact of grief. Different cultures have varying norms and practices for mourning, which can shape how family members express and process their grief. Understanding and respecting these cultural differences is important for creating an inclusive and supportive environment.

Think about a family from a culture that values public mourning might hold a community memorial service to honour the deceased parent. This service provides an opportunity for family members and the community to come together, share their grief, and celebrate the life of the parent.

Professional support, such as family therapy or counselling, can be invaluable in addressing the intergenerational impact of grief. These professionals can help families navigate the complex dynamics and emotions that arise from the loss of a parent. Therapy can provide tools for effective communication, conflict resolution, and emotional support, helping families to heal together.

A family who loses their patriarch might struggle with unresolved conflicts and differing grieving styles. By seeking family therapy, they can address these issues in a safe and supportive environment, finding ways to support each other and honour their father's memory.

The intergenerational impact of losing a parent is multifaceted, affecting each family member in unique ways. By acknowledging and addressing this impact, families can create a supportive and healing environment. Honouring the memory of the deceased parent through traditions, open communication, and professional support can help families navigate their grief together, fostering resilience and connection across generations.

Personal Growth Through Grief

Grieving the loss of a parent can be an incredibly transformative experience, often leading to significant personal growth. While the pain of loss is profound, it can also catalyse self-discovery, resilience, and a deeper understanding of one's own values and priorities. Embracing this potential for growth can help individuals navigate their grief with a sense of purpose and hope.

One of the first steps in experiencing personal growth through grief is acknowledging and accepting the full range of emotions that accompany loss. This means allowing oneself to feel sadness, anger, guilt, and confusion without judgment. These emotions are a natural part of the grieving process and can provide valuable insights into one's inner world.

The lady who loses her mother might initially feel overwhelmed by grief and anger. By allowing herself to fully experience these emotions and reflect on their origins, she gains a deeper understanding of her relationship with her mother and the aspects of their bond that she values most.

Engaging in self-reflection can be a powerful tool for personal growth. Taking time to explore personal values, beliefs, and goals can help individuals reconnect with themselves and discover new aspects of their identity. Journaling, meditating, or simply spending time in nature can provide the space needed for this introspection.

Think about a man who loses his father might find solace in hiking through the mountains his father loved. During these solitary walks, he reflects on his father's teachings and how they have shaped his own values and life choices. This reflection helps him reconnect with his sense of purpose and find new meaning in his life.

Grief can also inspire individuals to reevaluate their priorities and make positive changes in their lives. The loss of a parent can serve as a reminder of the impermanence of life, motivating individuals to pursue their passions, strengthen relationships, and focus on what truly matters. This shift in perspective can lead to a more fulfilling and intentional life.

Imagine a young woman who loses her father might decide to pursue a career change that aligns more closely with her passions and values. Inspired by her father's advice to follow her dreams, she takes the leap and finds greater satisfaction and purpose in her new path.

Finding ways to honour the memory of the deceased parent can also contribute to personal growth. Creating rituals, participating in activities they loved, or continuing their legacy through charitable work can provide a sense of connection and purpose. These acts of remembrance can help individuals integrate their parent's memory into their own lives, fostering a sense of continuity and meaning.

Think about a man who loses his mother might start a scholarship fund in her name, supporting students in a field she was passionate about. This act of service not only honours his mother's memory but also provides him with a sense of fulfilment and purpose.

Seeking support from friends, family, and professionals can facilitate personal growth through grief. Surrounding oneself with a supportive network provides validation, encouragement, and perspective. Therapy or counselling can offer tools for navigating the emotional complexities of grief and finding ways to grow through the experience.

The woman who loses her mother might seek therapy to address feelings of guilt and unresolved conflict. Through therapy, she gains insights into her emotions and develops healthier coping mechanisms. This process helps her grow emotionally and build stronger, more authentic relationships with others.

Engaging in creative expression can also be a valuable outlet for personal growth. Writing, painting, music, or other forms of art can provide a way to process emotions and explore new facets of one's identity. These creative activities can be therapeutic, allowing individuals to express their grief and discover new sources of strength and inspiration.

Think about a man who loses his father might take up photography, capturing images that reflect his journey through grief. This creative expression helps him process his emotions and see the world through a new lens, fostering personal growth and resilience.

Personal growth through grief is a deeply individual journey that requires patience, self-compassion, and openness to change. By acknowledging and exploring their emotions, reevaluating priorities, and seeking support, individuals can navigate the complexities of grief and emerge with a deeper understanding of themselves and their place in the world. The loss of a parent, while profoundly painful, can also be a catalyst for meaningful growth and transformation.

Finding Peace

Finding peace after the loss of a parent is a gradual and deeply personal journey. It involves navigating the intense emotions of grief, honouring the memory of the parent, and ultimately discovering a sense of acceptance and tranquillity. While the pain of loss may never completely disappear, it is possible to find moments of peace and healing.

One of the first steps towards finding peace is acknowledging and accepting the full range of emotions that accompany grief. This means allowing oneself to feel sadness, anger, guilt, and even relief without judgment. Embracing these emotions can provide a sense of release and help facilitate the healing process.

A woman who loses her mother might feel a mix of deep sorrow and relief that her mother is no longer suffering from a prolonged illness. By accepting these complex emotions, she can begin to process her grief and move towards a place of peace.

Creating rituals and routines that honour the memory of the parent can provide comfort and a sense of connection. These rituals can be simple or elaborate, depending on what feels meaningful. Lighting a candle, saying a prayer, or visiting a special place can serve as acts of remembrance and provide a sense of continuity.

Think about a man who loses his father might light a candle each evening and spend a few moments in quiet reflection. This daily ritual helps him feel connected to his father's memory and provides a sense of peace and solace.

Engaging in activities that bring joy and fulfilment can also help find peace. Pursuing hobbies, spending time in nature, and connecting with loved ones can provide moments of happiness and distraction from the intensity of grief. These activities can remind individuals that life, despite the loss, still holds beauty and meaning.

The lady who loses her mother might find joy in gardening, a hobby they both shared. Tending to her garden brings her comfort and a sense of connection to her mother, providing moments of peace amidst her grief.

Mindfulness and meditation practices can be powerful tools for finding peace. These practices encourage being present in the moment, accepting emotions without judgment, and cultivating a sense of calm. Mindfulness can help reduce anxiety and stress, providing a sense of tranquillity even amid grief.

Again, Think about a man who loses his father might practice mindfulness meditation each morning, focusing on his breath and observing his thoughts and emotions without judgment. This practice helps him stay grounded and find a sense of inner peace.

Seeking support from friends, family, and professionals can also facilitate finding peace. Surrounding oneself with a supportive network provides validation, encouragement, and perspective. Therapy or counselling can offer tools for navigating the emotional complexities of grief and finding ways to heal.

Imagine a woman who loses her mother might seek therapy to address feelings of guilt and unresolved conflict. Through therapy, she gains insights into her emotions and develops healthier coping mechanisms. This process helps her find peace and build stronger, more authentic relationships with others.

Finding peace also involves forgiving oneself and others. Grief can bring up feelings of guilt, regret, and anger. It is important to work through these emotions and find a way to forgive oneself for perceived shortcomings or unresolved conflicts. This forgiveness can provide a sense of release and pave the way towards peace.

Take, Imagine a man who loses his father might struggle

with feelings of guilt for not spending more time with him. Through therapy and self-reflection, he learns to forgive himself and focus on the positive memories and the love they shared. This forgiveness brings him a sense of peace and closure.

Ultimately, finding peace after the loss of a parent involves a combination of acknowledging emotions, honouring memories, engaging in fulfilling activities, and seeking support. It is a gradual process that requires patience, self-compassion, and openness to healing. While the pain of loss may never completely disappear, it is possible to find moments of peace and tranquillity, allowing for a renewed sense of hope and meaning in life.

Personal Story - Amina's Healing

Amina sat on the porch of her childhood home, the soft breeze carrying the scent of blooming jasmine from the garden her mother had tended with so much love. It had been two years since her mother passed away, yet the pain still felt fresh, a constant ache in her heart. Amina's journey through grief had been filled with sorrow, but also moments of healing, connection, and newfound strength.

In the immediate aftermath of her mother's death, Amina felt as though her world had been turned upside down. The routines and rituals that had once brought comfort now seemed hollow and empty. Making tea in the morning, a ritual she had shared with her mother, brought tears to her eyes. The house, filled with memories of her mother's laughter and warmth, felt unbearably silent.

Recognizing the need for support, Amina reached out to a grief counsellor. In the safe space of her counsellor's office, Amina began to explore the depths of her sorrow. Her counsellor introduced her to mindfulness and meditation, practices that helped her stay present and manage her overwhelming emotions. Through therapy, Amina learned to navigate the complexities of her grief and develop healthy coping strategies.

One of the most significant steps in Amina's healing journey was creating rituals to honour her mother's memory. Each morning, she would sit in her mother's garden, sipping tea and reflecting on their time together. This daily ritual provided a structured time for Amina to connect with her emotions and honour her mother's legacy. The garden, filled with her mother's favourite flowers, became a sanctuary of solace and reflection.

Amina also found solace in creative expression. She began to write letters to her mother, expressing her thoughts and feelings. These letters became a cherished collection, a testament to their bond and her journey through grief. Writing allowed Amina to process her emotions in a tangible and meaningful way, providing a sense of release and connection.

To further honour her mother's memory, Amina decided to start a community garden in her neighbourhood. This garden, open to all, would serve as a place of beauty, connection, and healing. She rallied her neighbours, sharing her vision and inviting them to contribute. Together, they transformed a vacant lot into a vibrant garden filled with flowers, vegetables, and seating areas for reflection. The community garden became a living tribute to her mother's love for gardening and brought joy and connection to the neighbourhood.

As she continued to heal, Amina set new goals for herself. She decided to pursue further education, enrolling in courses that aligned with her passion for environmental science. Inspired by her mother's love for nature, Amina focused on sustainability and conservation. This pursuit provided a sense of purpose and fulfilment, allowing Amina to channel her grief into positive action.

Maintaining connections with friends and family was also crucial for Amina's recovery. She communicated her needs openly, allowing her loved ones to understand how to best support her. These relationships provided ongoing support and encouragement, helping Amina navigate the ups and downs of her grief. Sharing stories and memories of her mother with family members created a sense of continuity and kept her mother's spirit alive.

Amina also sought connection with others who understood her pain. She joined a support group for adults who had lost parents, where she found a community of individuals who shared similar experiences. The group provided a space for Amina to share her story and connect with others who validated her grief. These connections offered comfort and understanding, helping Amina feel less alone in her journey.

Through these small but significant steps, Amina found a path towards healing. She learned to live with her grief, understanding that it was a part of her but not all of her. She embraced the support of her loved ones, found fulfilment in creative expression and community projects, and created new traditions that honoured her mother's memory.

Amina's journey through grief is a testament to the power of resilience, support, and self-discovery. Her story illustrates that while the pain of loss may never completely disappear, it is possible to find hope, meaning, and a renewed sense of purpose. By taking small steps towards healing and embracing new opportunities, Amina transformed her grief into a source of strength and continued to live a life filled with love and fulfilment.

CHAPTER 11: GRIEVING THE LOSS OF A SIBLING

The Unique Bond of Siblings

The bond between siblings is one of the most unique and enduring relationships in our lives. Siblings share a lifetime of memories, experiences, and mutual understanding that often transcends the typical dynamics of friendship and familial ties. Losing a sibling can be a deeply painful and complex experience, as it not only involves the loss of a loved one but also the loss of a shared history and future.

Siblings are often each other's first companions, playmates, and confidantes. They grow up together, navigating childhood, adolescence, and adulthood side by side. This shared journey creates a profound connection built on a foundation of mutual support, rivalry, and unconditional love. When a sibling dies, the surviving siblings are left to grapple with a void that feels impossible to fill.

One of the most challenging aspects of sibling grief is the sense of losing a part of oneself. Siblings often play a significant role in shaping each other's identities, and their absence can leave the surviving siblings feeling incomplete. This loss can be especially difficult to process, as it disrupts the continuity of the shared life story and future plans.

Imagine one who loses his younger brother might struggle with the absence of their shared dreams and aspirations. They had planned to start a business together, and now, the future they envisioned seems distant and unattainable. The loss of these shared dreams adds another layer of grief to his experience.

The intensity of sibling grief can also be compounded by the unique dynamics of sibling relationships. Sibling bonds can be complex, marked by periods of closeness and distance, harmony and conflict. The loss of a sibling can bring up unresolved issues and regrets, adding to the emotional burden. It is important to address these feelings and find ways to process them constructively.

Engaging in self-reflection and seeking professional support can help navigate these complex emotions. Therapy can provide a safe space to explore unresolved issues, work through feelings of guilt and regret, and develop healthy coping strategies. Think about a woman who loses her sister might seek therapy to address lingering feelings of resentment and guilt, finding a way to heal and move forward.

The death of a sibling can also affect family dynamics, as each family member processes their grief differently. Parents may be overwhelmed by their own sorrow, making it difficult to support the surviving siblings. Siblings may feel isolated in their grief, unsure of how to express their emotions or seek comfort. Open communication and mutual support within the family are crucial for navigating this difficult time.

A family who loses a daughter might struggle with their individual and collective grief. By holding regular family meetings where they share their feelings and memories, they create a supportive environment that fosters healing and connection. This open communication helps each family member feel validated and understood.

Finding ways to honour the memory of the sibling can provide comfort and a sense of connection. Creating rituals and traditions that celebrate their life and legacy can help keep their memory alive. This might involve setting up a small shrine with photographs and mementoes, writing letters to them, or participating in activities that were meaningful to them.

Think about the woman who loses her brother might create a memory box filled with his favourite items, letters, and photographs. Each year on his birthday, she takes time to reflect on their memories and share stories with her family. This ritual provides a sense of continuity and helps keep his memory alive.

Maintaining connections with friends and support groups can also be valuable. Sharing memories and stories with loved ones can help keep the sibling's legacy alive and provide a sense of comfort and belonging. Support groups for those who have lost siblings can offer a space to connect with others who understand the unique challenges of sibling grief.

The man who loses his sister might find solace in

joining a support group for adults who have lost siblings. Through the group, he connects with others who share their experiences and offer support. These connections provide validation and understanding, helping him feel less alone in his grief.

Engaging in activities that bring joy and fulfilment can also help in the healing process. Pursuing hobbies, spending time in nature, and connecting with loved ones can provide moments of happiness and distraction from the intensity of grief. These activities can remind individuals that life, despite the loss, still holds beauty and meaning.

Imagine a woman who loses her brother might find joy in painting, a hobby they both enjoyed. Creating art allows her to express her emotions and find solace in the process. Each painting becomes a tribute to their bond and a step towards healing.

The journey of sibling grief is deeply personal and multifaceted. By acknowledging the depth of the loss, seeking support, and finding meaningful ways to honour the sibling's memory, individuals can navigate this difficult journey and find moments of healing and hope. The unique bond of siblings, while profoundly altered by loss, can continue to provide strength and connection as they move forward.

Navigating Family Dynamics

The loss of a sibling can significantly impact family dynamics, creating a ripple effect that touches each family member in unique ways. Navigating these changes requires open communication, mutual support, and a willingness to adapt to new roles and responsibilities. Understanding and addressing the complexities of family dynamics can help families support each other through the grieving process and find a path towards healing together.

When a sibling dies, the surviving family members are left to cope with their individual grief while also managing the collective sorrow of the family. Each person's grief journey is unique, influenced by their relationship with the deceased, their personality, and their coping mechanisms. These differences can sometimes lead to misunderstandings and conflicts within the family.

One of the most important aspects of navigating family dynamics after the loss of a sibling is maintaining open and honest communication. Creating a safe space where family members can express their feelings, share memories, and support each other can foster understanding and connection. Family meetings, regular check-ins, or informal gatherings can provide opportunities for these conversations.

The family who loses a son might struggle with how to communicate their grief. By setting aside time each week for a family meeting, they create a structured space where everyone can share their emotions and offer support. These meetings help the family stay connected and navigate their grief together.

The loss of a sibling can also lead to shifts in family roles and responsibilities. Surviving siblings may find themselves taking on new roles, such as supporting grieving parents or stepping into the role of the eldest sibling. These changes can be challenging and may require time to adjust. It is important to recognize these shifts and provide support and understanding as family members navigate their new roles.

After the death of their eldest brother, a younger sister might feel the pressure to fill his shoes. She may take on additional responsibilities to support her parents and siblings, leading to feelings of overwhelm and stress. By openly discussing these changes and seeking support, the family can work together to share the burden and ensure that everyone feels supported.

Grief can also bring up unresolved issues and conflicts within the family. Past disagreements or misunderstandings may resurface, adding to the emotional strain. Addressing these issues with compassion and a willingness to listen can help heal old wounds and strengthen family bonds. Seeking professional support, such as family therapy, can provide tools for effective communication and conflict resolution.

A family that loses a daughter might find that old sibling rivalries resurface, leading to tension and conflict. By seeking family therapy, they can work through these issues in a safe and supportive environment, finding ways to support each other and honour their daughter's memory.

Cultural and societal expectations around grief can also influence family dynamics. Different cultures have varying norms and practices for mourning, which can shape how family members express and process their grief. Understanding and respecting these cultural differences is important for creating an inclusive and supportive environment.

A family from a culture that values public mourning might hold a community memorial service to honour their deceased sibling. This service provides an opportunity for family members and the community to come together, share their grief, and celebrate the life of the sibling.

Finding ways to honour the memory of the sibling can also help navigate family dynamics. Creating rituals and traditions that celebrate their life and legacy can provide comfort and a sense of connection. This might involve setting up a small shrine with photographs and mementoes, writing letters to them, or participating in activities that were meaningful to them.

The family who loses a son might create a scholarship fund in his name, supporting students in a field he was passionate about. This act of service not only honours his memory but also provides the family with a sense of purpose and fulfilment.

Maintaining connections with friends and support groups can also provide valuable support. Sharing memories and stories with loved ones can help keep the sibling's legacy alive and provide a sense of comfort and belonging. Support groups for those who have lost siblings can offer a space to connect with others who understand the unique challenges of sibling grief.

Imagine a woman who loses her sister might find solace in joining a support group for adults who have lost siblings. Through the group, she connects with others who share their experiences and offer support. These connections provide validation and understanding, helping her feel less alone in her grief.

Navigating family dynamics after the loss of a sibling is a complex and ongoing process. By maintaining open communication, supporting each other through role changes, and finding meaningful ways to honour the sibling's memory, families can navigate this difficult journey together. The strength and resilience of the family unit can provide a foundation for healing and connection as they move forward.

Personal Story - Elena's Journey

Elena sat in her brother's old room, the walls still adorned with posters of his favourite bands and sports teams. It had been a year since Marco passed away, and the pain of his loss was still a constant presence in her life. Elena's journey through grief had been marked by deep sorrow, but also moments of connection, resilience, and growth.

In the immediate aftermath of Marco's death, Elena felt as though her world had been shattered. The routines and rituals they had shared as siblings now felt empty and meaningless. Walking past his room each day was a painful reminder of his absence. Elena struggled to find her footing, feeling lost and disconnected from the world around her.

Recognizing the need for support, Elena reached out to a grief counsellor. In the safe space of her counsellor's office, Elena began to explore the depths of her sorrow. Her counsellor introduced her to mindfulness and meditation, practices that helped her stay present and manage her overwhelming emotions. Through therapy, Elena learned to navigate the complexities of her grief and develop healthy coping strategies.

One of the most significant steps in Elena's healing journey was creating rituals to honour Marco's memory. Each evening, she would light a candle in his room and spend a few moments reflecting on their time together. This daily ritual provided a structured time for Elena to connect with her emotions and honour Marco's legacy. The soft glow of the candle brought her a sense of peace and connection.

Elena also found solace in creative expression. She began to write letters to Marco, expressing her thoughts and feelings. These letters became a cherished collection, a testament to their bond and her journey through grief. Writing allowed Elena to process her emotions in a tangible and meaningful way, providing a sense of release and connection.

To further honour Marco's memory, Elena decided to start a charity in his name. Marco had been passionate about helping others, and Elena wanted to continue his legacy of kindness and generosity. She organized community events and fundraisers, channelling her grief into positive action. The charity became a living tribute to Marco's spirit and brought joy and connection to the community.

As she continued to heal, Elena set new goals for herself. She decided to pursue further education, enrolling in courses that aligned with her passion for social work. Inspired by Marco's compassion and dedication to helping others, Elena focused on making a difference in the lives of those in need. This pursuit provided a sense of purpose and fulfilment, allowing Elena to channel her grief into positive action.

Maintaining connections with friends and family was also crucial for Elena's recovery. She communicated her needs openly, allowing her loved ones to understand how to best support her. These relationships provided ongoing support and encouragement, helping Elena navigate the ups and downs of her grief. Sharing stories and memories of Marco with family members created a sense of continuity and kept his spirit alive.

Elena also sought connection with others who understood her pain. She joined a support group for adults who had lost siblings, where she found a community of individuals who shared similar experiences. The group provided a space for Elena to share her story and connect with others who validated her grief. These connections offered comfort and understanding, helping Elena feel less alone in her journey.

Through these small but significant steps, Elena found a path towards healing. She learned to live with her grief, understanding that it was a part of her but not all of her. She embraced the support of her loved ones, found fulfilment in creative expression and community service, and created new traditions that honoured Marco's memory.

Elena's journey through grief is a testament to the power of resilience, support, and self-discovery. Her story illustrates that while the pain of loss may never completely disappear, it is possible to find hope, meaning, and a renewed sense of purpose. By taking small steps towards healing and embracing new opportunities, Elena transformed her grief into a source of strength and continued to live a life filled with love and fulfilment.

Grieving the Loss of a Friend

The loss of a close friend can be an incredibly painful and isolating experience. Friends often play a significant role in our lives, providing companionship, support, and a sense of belonging. Losing a friend can leave a void that feels difficult to fill, as well as a profound sense of loneliness and grief. Understanding and navigating this unique form of loss is essential for finding a path towards healing and connection.

Friendships are built on mutual trust, shared experiences, and deep emotional bonds. Friends are often the people we turn to in times of joy and sorrow, the ones who understand us in ways that others may not. When a friend dies, the loss can feel like losing a part of oneself, as well as the future experiences and memories that were yet to be made.

One of the most challenging aspects of grieving the loss of a friend is the sense of isolation that can accompany it. Friends often occupy a unique space in our lives that is different from family or romantic relationships. The loss of a friend may not always be recognized or validated by others, leading to feelings of loneliness and misunderstanding.

Imagine a woman who loses her best friend might find that her grief is not fully acknowledged by her family or coworkers. She may feel isolated in her sorrow, unsure of how to express the depth of her loss. It is important to seek out support from those who understand and validate the significance of the friendship.

Maintaining open communication with mutual friends can provide a sense of connection and understanding. Sharing memories, stories, and feelings with those who also knew and loved the deceased friend can help keep their memory alive and provide comfort. These shared connections can offer a sense of solidarity and support.

Think about a group of friends who lose one of their own might come together to share stories and memories, creating a space where they can grieve and heal together. These gatherings provide a sense of community and help keep the friend's spirit alive.

Engaging in rituals and activities that honour the friend's memory can provide comfort and a sense of connection. This might involve setting up a small shrine with photographs and mementos, writing letters to them, or participating in activities that were meaningful to them. These acts of remembrance can help integrate the memory of the friend into daily life and provide a source of solace.

Imagine a man who loses his close friend might create a playlist of their favourite songs, listening to it whenever he wants to feel connected to his friend. This ritual provides a sense of continuity and helps keep the friend's memory alive.

Seeking professional support from a therapist or grief counsellor can provide additional tools and strategies for navigating the loss of a friend. Therapy can offer a safe space to explore complex emotions, develop healthy coping mechanisms, and find ways to move forward. Support groups for those who have lost friends can also offer a space to connect with others who understand the unique challenges of this type of grief.

Think about a woman who loses her friend might seek therapy to address feelings of guilt and unresolved conflict. Through therapy, she gains insights into her emotions and develops healthier coping mechanisms. This process helps her find peace and build stronger, more authentic relationships with others.

Engaging in activities that bring joy and fulfilment can also help in the healing process. Pursuing hobbies, spending time in nature, and connecting with loved ones can provide moments of happiness and distraction from the intensity of grief. These activities can remind individuals that life, despite the loss, still holds beauty and meaning.

Imagine a man who loses his best friend might find joy in hiking, a hobby they both enjoyed. Exploring new trails and spending time in nature brings him comfort and a sense of connection to his friend's memory.

Finding ways to continue the friend's legacy can provide a sense of purpose and fulfilment. This might involve supporting a cause they were passionate about, volunteering in their honour, or creating something that reflects their values and spirit. These acts of service can help transform grief into positive action and keep the friend's memory alive.

Imagine a woman who loses her friend might start a charity event in their honour, raising funds for a cause they both cared about. This act of service not only honours her friend's memory but also provides her with a sense of purpose and fulfilment.

Grieving the loss of a friend is a deeply personal and complex experience. By acknowledging the depth of the loss, seeking support, and finding meaningful ways to honour the friend's memory, individuals can navigate this difficult journey and find moments of healing and hope. The bond of friendship, while profoundly altered by loss, can continue to provide strength and connection as they move forward.

Personal Story - Liam's Friendship

Liam stood by the riverbank, the place where he and his best friend, Alex, had spent countless hours fishing, talking, and dreaming about the future. It had been a year since Alex passed away, and the pain of his loss still felt raw and overwhelming. Liam's journey through grief had been marked by deep sorrow, but also moments of connection, resilience, and personal growth.

In the immediate aftermath of Alex's death, Liam felt as though his world had come to a standstill. The routines and rituals they had shared as friends now felt empty and meaningless. The riverbank, once a place of joy and camaraderie, now seemed like a stark reminder of his absence. Liam struggled to find his footing, feeling lost and disconnected from the world around him.

Recognizing the need for support, Liam reached out to a grief counsellor. In the safe space of his counsellor's office, Liam began to explore the depths of his sorrow. His counsellor introduced him to mindfulness and meditation, practices that helped him stay present and manage his overwhelming emotions. Through therapy, Liam learned to navigate the complexities of his grief and develop healthy coping strategies.

One of the most significant steps in Liam's healing journey was creating rituals to honour Alex's memory. Each weekend, he would visit the riverbank, bringing along Alex's favourite fishing rod. He would sit quietly by the water, reflecting on their time together and the memories they had shared. This ritual provided a structured time for Liam to connect with his emotions and honour Alex's legacy. The serene surroundings of the riverbank brought him a sense of peace and connection.

Liam also found solace in creative expression. He began to write letters to Alex, expressing his thoughts and feelings. These letters became a cherished collection, a testament to their bond and his journey through grief. Writing allowed Liam to process his emotions in a tangible and meaningful way, providing a sense of release and connection.

To further honour Alex's memory, Liam decided to start a community fishing event in his honour. Alex had been passionate about fishing and loved teaching others the craft. Liam organized the event, inviting friends, family, and community members to participate. The event became a living tribute to Alex's spirit and brought joy and connection to the community.

As he continued to heal, Liam set new goals for himself. He decided to pursue further education, enrolling in courses that aligned with his passion for environmental science. Inspired by Alex's love for nature, Liam focused on sustainability and conservation. This pursuit provided a sense of purpose and fulfilment, allowing Liam to channel his grief into positive action.

Maintaining connections with mutual friends and family was also crucial for Liam's recovery. He communicated his needs openly, allowing his loved ones to understand how to best support him. These relationships provided ongoing support and encouragement, helping Liam navigate the ups and downs of his grief. Sharing stories and memories of Alex with mutual friends created a sense of continuity and kept his spirit alive.

Liam also sought connection with others who understood his pain. He joined a support group for adults who had lost friends, where he found a community of individuals who shared similar experiences. The group provided a space for Liam to share his story and connect with others who validated his grief. These connections offered comfort and understanding, helping Liam feel less alone in his journey.

Through these small but significant steps, Liam found a path towards healing. He learned to live with his grief, understanding that it was a part of him but not all of him. He embraced the support of his loved ones, found fulfilment in creative expression and community service, and created new traditions that honoured Alex's memory.

Liam's journey through grief is a testament to the power of resilience, support, and self-discovery. His story illustrates that while the pain of loss may never completely disappear, it is possible to find hope, meaning, and a renewed sense of purpose. By taking small steps towards healing and embracing new opportunities, Liam transformed his grief into a source of strength and continued to live a life filled with love and fulfilment.

CHAPTER 12: GRIEVING THE LOSS OF A PET

The Deep Bond with Pets

The bond between humans and their pets is profound and unique, often marked by unconditional love, companionship, and mutual support. Pets become integral members of the family, providing comfort and joy through their unwavering presence. When a pet dies, the loss can be devastating, leaving a significant void in the lives of their human companions. Understanding and honouring this bond is essential for navigating the grief that follows the loss of a beloved pet.

Pets offer a type of companionship that is unlike any other. They are constant, loyal, and non-judgmental, offering solace during times of stress and joy during moments of happiness. The routines and rituals shared with pets, such as daily walks, feeding times, and play sessions, create a strong sense of connection and dependence. When a pet dies, these routines are abruptly interrupted, leaving their human companions grappling with a deep sense of loss and disorientation.

One of the most challenging aspects of grieving the loss of a pet is the societal tendency to minimize this type of grief. Friends, family, and colleagues may not always understand the depth of the bond shared with a pet, leading to feelings of isolation and misunderstanding. It is important to seek out support from those who validate and understand the significance of this loss.

The woman who loses her dog might find that her coworkers do not fully appreciate her grief. She seeks support from fellow pet owners who understand the profound bond between humans and their pets. These connections provide validation and comfort, helping her navigate her sorrow.

Engaging in rituals and activities that honour the pet's memory can provide comfort and a sense of connection. This might involve creating a memorial, writing letters to the pet, or participating in activities that were meaningful to them. These acts of remembrance can help integrate the memory of the pet into daily life and provide a source of solace.

Think about a man who loses his cat might create a small garden in his backyard, planting flowers and herbs that his cat loved to explore. This garden becomes a living tribute to his pet's memory and a place where he can reflect and find peace.

Maintaining open communication with family and friends about the loss can also provide a sense of support and understanding. Sharing memories, stories, and feelings with loved ones can help keep the pet's memory alive and provide comfort. These shared connections can offer a sense of solidarity and support.

Imagine a family who loses their pet might come together to create a scrapbook filled with photographs, drawings, and stories about their pet. This project allows each family member to express their grief and celebrate the joy their pet brought into their lives.

Seeking professional support from a therapist or grief counsellor can provide additional tools and strategies for navigating the loss of a pet. Therapy can offer a safe space to explore complex emotions, develop healthy coping mechanisms, and find ways to move forward. Support groups for those who have lost pets can also offer a space to connect with others who understand the unique challenges of this type of grief.

Think about a woman who loses her rabbit might seek therapy to address feelings of guilt and sadness. Through therapy, she gains insights into her emotions and develops healthier coping mechanisms. This process helps her find peace and build stronger, more authentic relationships with others.

Engaging in activities that bring joy and fulfilment can also help in the healing process. Pursuing hobbies, spending time in nature, and connecting with loved ones can provide moments of happiness and distraction from the intensity of grief. These activities can remind individuals that life, despite the loss, still holds beauty and meaning.

Imagine a man who loses his dog might find joy in hiking, a hobby they both enjoyed. Exploring new trails and spending time in nature brings him comfort and a sense of connection to his pet's memory.

Finding ways to continue the pet's legacy can provide a sense of purpose and fulfilment. This might involve supporting a cause related to animal welfare, volunteering at a local shelter, or creating something that reflects their values and spirit. These acts of service can help transform grief into positive action and keep the pet's memory alive.

Imagine a woman who loses her bird might start a birdwatching club in her community, sharing her love for birds with others and raising awareness about bird conservation. This act of service not only honours her pet's memory but also provides her with a sense of purpose and fulfilment.

Grieving the loss of a pet is a deeply personal and complex experience. By acknowledging the depth of the loss, seeking support, and finding meaningful ways to honour the pet's memory, individuals can navigate this difficult journey and find moments of healing and hope. The bond with pets, while profoundly altered by loss, can continue to provide strength and connection as they move forward.

Personal Story - Emma's Companion

Emma sat on the porch of her house, the place where she and her dog, Max, had spent countless hours together. It had been six months since Max passed away, and the pain of his loss was still a constant presence in her life. Emma's journey through grief had been marked by deep sorrow, but also moments of connection, resilience, and growth.

In the immediate aftermath of Max's death, Emma felt as

though her world had lost its colour. The routines and rituals they had shared, such as their morning walks and playtime in the yard, now felt empty and meaningless. The house, once filled with Max's joyful energy, now seemed silent and lonely. Emma struggled to find her footing, feeling lost and disconnected from the world around her.

Recognizing the need for support, Emma reached out to a grief counsellor. In the safe space of her counsellor's office, Emma began to explore the depths of her sorrow. Her counsellor introduced her to mindfulness and meditation, practices that helped her stay present and manage her overwhelming emotions. Through therapy, Emma learned to navigate the complexities of her grief and develop healthy coping strategies.

One of the most significant steps in Emma's healing journey was creating rituals to honour Max's memory. Each morning, she would take a walk along their favourite trail, carrying a small memento of Max—a collar charm that had once jingled with each step he took. This ritual provided a structured time for Emma to connect with her emotions and honour Max's legacy. The familiar sights and sounds of the trail brought her a sense of peace and connection.

Emma also found solace in creative expression. She began to write letters to Max, expressing her thoughts and feelings. These letters became a cherished collection, a testament to their bond and her journey through grief. Writing allowed Emma to process her emotions in a tangible and meaningful way, providing a sense of release and connection.

To further honour Max's memory, Emma decided to volunteer at a local animal shelter. Max had always been a friendly and loving dog, and Emma wanted to continue his legacy of kindness and companionship. She spent her weekends walking the shelter dogs, offering them the same love and care that Max had given her. Volunteering became a living tribute to Max's spirit and brought joy and connection to Emma's life.

As she continued to heal, Emma set new goals for herself. She decided to adopt another dog, a rescue named Daisy. Emma knew that Daisy could never replace Max, but she hoped to provide her with the same love and care. Daisy brought new energy and joy into Emma's life, helping her find a renewed sense of purpose and fulfilment.

Maintaining connections with friends and family was also crucial for Emma's recovery. She communicated her needs openly, allowing her loved ones to understand how to best support her. These relationships provided ongoing support and encouragement, helping Emma navigate the ups and downs of her grief. Sharing stories and memories of Max with friends and family created a sense of continuity and kept his spirit alive.

Emma also sought connection with others who understood her pain. She joined a support group for pet owners who had lost their companions, where she found a community of individuals who shared similar experiences. The group provided a space for Emma to share her story and connect with others who validated her grief. These connections offered comfort and understanding, helping Emma feel less alone in her journey.

Through these small but significant steps, Emma found a path towards healing. She learned to live with her grief, understanding that it was a part of her but not all of her. She embraced the support of her loved ones, found fulfilment in creative expression and volunteering, and created new traditions that honoured Max's memory.

Emma's journey through grief is a testament to the power of resilience, support, and self-discovery. Her story illustrates that while the pain of loss may never completely disappear, it is possible to find hope, meaning, and a renewed sense of purpose. By taking small steps towards healing and embracing new opportunities, Emma transformed her grief into a source of strength and continued to live a life filled with love and fulfilment.

CHAPTER 13: RESOURCES FOR COPING WITH GRIEF

Professional Support

Coping with grief can be an overwhelming and isolating experience. Professional support, such as therapy, counselling, and support groups, can provide invaluable resources for navigating the complexities of grief and finding a path towards healing. Understanding the various forms of professional support available can help individuals make informed decisions about the best options for their unique needs.

1. Grief Counselling and Therapy: Grief counsellors and therapists are trained professionals who specialize in helping individuals cope with loss. They provide a safe and confidential space to explore emotions, process grief, and develop healthy coping strategies. Therapy can be particularly beneficial for those experiencing intense or prolonged grief, unresolved conflicts, or difficulty functioning in daily life.

The young man who lost his spouse might seek grief counselling to address feelings of guilt and sadness. Through therapy, he gains insights into his emotions and develops healthier coping mechanisms, helping him navigate his grief and find a sense of peace.

2. Support Groups: Support groups offer a community of individuals who share similar experiences of loss. These groups provide a space to share stories, offer mutual support, and receive validation from others who understand the unique challenges of grief. Support groups can be found through local community centres, hospitals, religious organizations, and online platforms.

Think about a woman who loses her child might join a support group for bereaved parents. Through the group, she connects with others who share their experiences and offer support. These connections provide validation and understanding, helping her feel less alone in her grief.

3. Specialized Therapies: There are various specialized therapies that can be beneficial for coping with grief, including cognitive-behavioural therapy (CBT), art therapy, and mindfulness-based therapies. These approaches can help individuals process their emotions, challenge negative thought patterns, and find new ways to cope with their grief.

Imagine a teenager who loses a sibling might benefit from art therapy, where they can express their emotions through creative activities. This form of therapy provides a safe and non-verbal way to explore their grief and find healing.

4. Online Therapy and Support: Online therapy and support groups offer a convenient and accessible option for those who may have difficulty attending in-person sessions. Many therapists and counsellors offer virtual sessions, and there are numerous online support groups and forums where individuals can connect with others who understand their grief.

A person who lives in a remote area might find it challenging to access local support groups. By participating in an online support group, they can connect with others who share their experiences and receive support from the comfort of their own home.

5. Hospice and Bereavement Services: Hospice organizations often provide bereavement support for families and individuals who have lost a loved one. These services can include counselling, support groups, and educational resources to help individuals navigate the grieving process. Hospice bereavement services are typically available for a period after the death of a loved one, providing ongoing support as needed.

Imagine a family who loses a grandparent might receive bereavement support from a hospice organization. Through counselling and support groups, they can process their grief and find ways to honour their loved one's memory.

6. Religious and Spiritual Support: For many individuals, religious and spiritual beliefs play a significant role in coping with grief. Religious organizations often provide pastoral counselling, support groups, and rituals that can offer comfort and a sense of connection. Spiritual

practices, such as prayer, meditation, and attending religious services, can provide solace and guidance during the grieving process.

Think about a person who loses their partner might find comfort in attending religious services and participating in rituals that honour their partner's memory. These practices provide a sense of connection to their faith and community, helping them navigate their grief.

7. Books and Literature: There are numerous books and articles available on the topic of grief and loss. These resources can provide insights, comfort, and practical advice for coping with grief. Reading about others' experiences and learning about different coping strategies can help individuals feel less alone and more empowered in their grief journey.

Imagine a person who loses their parent might find solace in reading a memoir written by someone who has experienced a similar loss. The book provides validation and comfort, helping them feel understood and supported.

8. Helplines and Crisis Support: There are various helplines and crisis support services available for individuals experiencing intense grief or emotional distress. These services provide immediate support and resources for those in need. Helplines can offer a listening ear, crisis intervention, and referrals to additional support services.

The gentleman who feels overwhelmed by their grief might call a crisis helpline for immediate support and guidance. The helpline counsellor provides comfort and practical advice, helping them navigate their emotions and find additional resources for ongoing support.

Professional support can play a crucial role in helping individuals navigate the complexities of grief and find a path towards healing. By understanding the various forms of support available, individuals can make informed decisions about the best options for their unique needs. Seeking professional help is a courageous and important step in the journey of grief, offering the tools and support needed to find moments of peace and hope.

Self-Help Strategies

In addition to professional support, self-help strategies can be valuable tools for coping with grief and finding a path towards healing. These strategies empower individuals to take an active role in their grief journey, providing practical ways to manage emotions, reduce stress, and foster resilience. Here are some effective self-help strategies for navigating grief:

1. Journaling: Writing about your thoughts and feelings can be a powerful way to process grief and gain insights into your emotions. Keeping a journal allows you to express your feelings freely and without judgment, providing a safe space to explore your grief. Regular journaling can help you track your progress, identify patterns, and find moments of clarity.

The man who loses their sibling might keep a daily journal where they write about their memories, emotions, and reflections. This practice helps them process their grief and find a sense of release.

2. Mindfulness and Meditation: Mindfulness and meditation practices can help you stay present and manage overwhelming emotions. These practices encourage you to observe your thoughts and feelings without judgment, fostering a sense of acceptance and calm. Regular mindfulness and meditation can reduce stress, improve emotional regulation, and provide a sense of inner peace.

Think about a woman who loses her mother might practice mindfulness meditation each morning, focusing on her breath and observing her emotions. This practice helps her stay grounded and find a sense of tranquillity amidst her grief.

3. Physical Activity: Engaging in regular physical activity can provide numerous benefits for emotional and physical well-being. Exercise releases endorphins, which can improve mood and reduce stress. Activities such as walking, running, yoga, or dancing can provide a healthy outlet for emotions and a way to care for your body during the grieving process.

Imagine a man who loses his spouse might take up jogging, finding solace in the rhythmic movement and the sense of accomplishment it brings. Regular exercise helps him manage his emotions and maintain his physical health.

4. Creative Expression: Creative activities such as writing, painting, music, or crafting can provide a therapeutic outlet for emotions. These activities allow you to express your feelings in a non-verbal way and explore new facets of your identity. Creative expression can be a powerful

way to process grief and find moments of joy and fulfilment.

Think about a teenager who loses a friend might take up painting, using colours and shapes to express their emotions. This creative activity provides a sense of release and helps them navigate their grief.

5. Connecting with Nature: Spending time in nature can provide a sense of peace and perspective. Activities such as hiking, gardening, or simply sitting in a park can help you feel grounded and connected to the natural world. Nature can offer a sense of continuity and remind you of the cycles of life and renewal.

Imagine a woman who loses her partner might find comfort in gardening, planting flowers and tending to her garden. This activity provides a sense of connection to the earth and a way to honour her partner's memory.

6. Practicing Gratitude: Focusing on gratitude can help shift your perspective and find moments of positivity amidst grief. Reflecting on the things you are thankful for, no matter how small, can provide a sense of appreciation and hope. Keeping a gratitude journal or sharing moments of gratitude with others can reinforce this practice.

Think about a man who loses his father might keep a gratitude journal, writing down three things he is grateful for each day. This practice helps him find moments of positivity and maintain a hopeful outlook.

7. Creating Rituals: Establishing new rituals or maintaining existing ones can provide a sense of structure and continuity. Rituals such as lighting a

candle, saying a prayer, or visiting a special place can offer comfort and a way to honour the memory of your loved one. These acts of remembrance can provide a sense of connection and meaning.

Imagine a family who loses their pet might create a ritual of lighting a candle each evening and sharing a memory of their pet. This practice provides a sense of continuity and helps keep the pet's memory alive.

8. Seeking Social Support: Surrounding yourself with supportive friends and family can provide comfort and encouragement. Sharing your feelings and experiences with others who care about you can help you feel less alone and more understood. Building a network of support can provide valuable resources and emotional strength.

Think about a woman who loses her child might lean on her close friends for support, sharing her grief and finding comfort in their presence. These relationships provide a sense of community and understanding.

9. Setting Goals: Setting small, achievable goals can provide a sense of direction and accomplishment. These goals can be related to self-care, personal growth, or honouring the memory of your loved one. Achieving these goals can boost confidence and provide a sense of progress.

Imagine a person who loses their partner might set a goal to complete a creative project in their honour, such as creating a scrapbook or organizing a charity event. This goal provides a sense of purpose and fulfilment.

10. Engaging in Spiritual Practices: For many individuals,

spiritual beliefs and practices play a significant role in coping with grief. Engaging in spiritual activities such as prayer, meditation, attending religious services, or reading spiritual texts can provide comfort and a sense of connection. Spiritual practices can offer guidance and solace during the grieving process.

Think about a man who loses his mother might find comfort in attending weekly religious services and participating in community rituals. These practices provide a sense of connection to his faith and community, helping him navigate his grief.

Self-help strategies can empower individuals to take an active role in their grief journey, providing practical ways to manage emotions, reduce stress, and foster resilience. By incorporating these strategies into daily life, individuals can find moments of peace and healing, and gradually build a renewed sense of hope and purpose.

Community and Online Resources

In addition to professional support and self-help strategies, community and online resources can play a crucial role in helping individuals navigate their grief. These resources provide access to a wide range of support networks, educational materials, and coping tools that can be invaluable in the healing process. Here are some community and online resources for coping with grief:

1. Local Support Groups: Many communities offer in-person support groups for individuals experiencing grief. These groups provide a safe and supportive environment where individuals can share their stories, receive validation, and connect with others who understand

their pain. Local support groups can be found through community centres, hospitals, religious organizations, and mental health agencies.

Consider a woman who loses her husband, might join a local support group for widows. Through the group, she connects with other women who share similar experiences and offer mutual support. These connections provide a sense of community and help her feel less alone in her grief.

2. Online Support Communities: Online support communities offer a convenient and accessible option for those who may have difficulty attending in-person groups. These communities provide a platform for individuals to connect with others from around the world, share their experiences, and offer support. Online forums, social media groups, and specialized websites can provide valuable resources and a sense of connection.

Think about a man who loses his child might join an online forum for bereaved parents. Through the forum, he connects with other parents who understand his pain and offer advice and support. These online connections provide comfort and validation, helping him navigate his grief.

3. Grief and Loss Websites: Numerous websites are dedicated to providing information, resources, and support for individuals experiencing grief. These websites often include articles, videos, and personal stories that offer insights into the grieving process and practical advice for coping with loss. Many websites also offer directories of local and online support services.

Imagine a person who loses their sibling might visit a grief and loss website to read articles about sibling grief and find resources for support. The information and connections found on the website provide valuable guidance and comfort.

4. Educational Workshops and Webinars: Many organizations offer educational workshops and webinars on topics related to grief and loss. These events provide an opportunity to learn from experts, ask questions, and connect with others who are experiencing similar challenges. Workshops and webinars can cover a wide range of topics, including coping strategies, self-care, and specific types of loss.

Think about a woman who loses her father might attend a webinar on coping with parental grief. The webinar provides her with practical tools and strategies for managing her emotions, as well as an opportunity to connect with others who understand her experience.

5. Grief Counselling Services: Many communities offer grief counselling services through local mental health agencies, hospices, and religious organizations. These services provide access to trained professionals who can offer individual or group counselling sessions. Grief counselling services can be a valuable resource for those who need additional support in navigating their grief.

Imagine a family who loses their mother might seek grief counselling services through a local hospice organization. The counselling sessions provide them with a safe space to process their emotions and receive support from a trained professional.

6. Helplines and Crisis Support Services: Helplines and crisis support services offer immediate assistance for individuals experiencing intense grief or emotional distress. These services provide a listening ear, crisis intervention, and referrals to additional support services. Helplines can be particularly helpful for those who need immediate support outside of regular office hours.

Think about a person who feels overwhelmed by their grief might call a crisis helpline for immediate support and guidance. The helpline counsellor provides comfort and practical advice, helping them navigate their emotions and find additional resources for ongoing support.

7. Religious and Spiritual Organizations: Many religious and spiritual organizations offer support services for individuals experiencing grief. These services can include pastoral counselling, support groups, and rituals that provide comfort and a sense of connection. Spiritual practices, such as prayer, meditation, and attending religious services, can also offer solace and guidance during the grieving process.

Imagine a person who loses their partner might find comfort in attending religious services and participating in rituals that honour their partner's memory. These practices provide a sense of connection to their faith and community, helping them navigate their grief.

8. Grief and Bereavement Books: There are numerous books available on the topic of grief and loss, written by experts and individuals who have experienced grief themselves. These books can provide insights, comfort,

and practical advice for coping with grief. Reading about others' experiences and learning about different coping strategies can help individuals feel less alone and more empowered in their grief journey.

Imagine a woman who loses her child might find solace in reading a memoir written by someone who has experienced a similar loss. The book provides validation and comfort, helping her feel understood and supported.

9. Memorial and Tribute Services: Many communities offer memorial and tribute services for individuals who have lost a loved one. These services provide an opportunity to honour the memory of the deceased and connect with others who are experiencing similar losses. Memorial services can be a source of comfort and connection, providing a space to celebrate the life and legacy of the loved one.

Imagine a family who loses their father might participate in a community memorial service organized by a local hospice. The service provides an opportunity to share memories, celebrate their father's life, and connect with others who understand their grief.

10. Volunteer Opportunities: Engaging in volunteer work can be a meaningful way to channel grief into positive action. Many organizations offer volunteer opportunities that allow individuals to give back to their community and support others who are experiencing similar challenges. Volunteering can provide a sense of purpose and fulfilment, helping individuals find meaning and connection in the midst of their grief.

Think about a person who loses their pet might

volunteer at a local animal shelter, providing care and companionship to animals in need. This act of service not only honours their pet's memory but also provides them with a sense of purpose and fulfilment.

Community and online resources can provide valuable support and connection for individuals navigating the complexities of grief. By accessing these resources, individuals can find the tools, support networks, and guidance needed to navigate their grief journey and find moments of healing and hope.

Books and Literature

Books and literature can be a valuable source of comfort, guidance, and support for individuals navigating grief. Whether written by experts, individuals who have experienced loss, or fictional characters, these works can provide insights, validation, and practical advice for coping with grief. Here are some recommended books and literature for those seeking support in their grief journey:

1. "On Grief and Grieving" by Elisabeth Kübler-Ross and David Kessler: This classic book explores the five stages of grief—denial, anger, bargaining, depression, and acceptance—providing a framework for understanding the emotional journey of grief. Written by renowned grief experts, this book offers compassionate insights and practical advice for navigating the complexities of loss.

Imagine a person who loses their spouse might find comfort in reading "On Grief and Grieving," gaining a deeper understanding of their emotions and finding practical tools for coping.

2. "The Year of Magical Thinking" by Joan Didion: In this memoir, Joan Didion recounts her experiences of grief following the sudden death of her husband. With raw honesty and poignant reflection, Didion explores the impact of loss and the process of finding a new normal. This book offers a deeply personal and relatable perspective on grief.

Think about a woman who loses her husband might find solace in reading "The Year of Magical Thinking," connecting with Didion's journey and finding validation for her own experiences.

3. "Grief Counselling and Grief Therapy" by J. William Worden: This comprehensive guide provides an overview of the principles and practices of grief counselling. Written for both professionals and individuals seeking support, this book offers practical strategies for understanding and navigating grief. It includes case studies and real-life examples to illustrate key concepts.

Imagine a therapist working with grieving clients might use "Grief Counselling and Grief Therapy" as a resource to enhance their practice and provide effective support.

4. "Healing After Loss: Daily Meditations for Working Through Grief" by Martha Whitmore Hickman: This book offers daily meditations and reflections for those coping with grief. Each entry provides a thoughtful message, offering comfort, inspiration, and practical advice. The daily format makes it an accessible and supportive companion for the grieving process.

Think about a person who loses their parent might incorporate "Healing After Loss" into their daily routine, finding solace and guidance in the meditations.

5. "A Grief Observed" by C.S. Lewis: In this classic work, C.S. Lewis reflects on his grief following the death of his wife. With profound honesty and vulnerability, Lewis explores the depths of his sorrow and the struggle to find meaning in the midst of loss. This book offers a deeply personal and philosophical perspective on grief.

Imagine a man who loses his partner might find comfort in reading "A Grief Observed," connecting with Lewis's reflections and finding validation for his own experiences.

6. "It's OK That You're Not OK: Meeting Grief and Loss in a Culture That Doesn't Understand" by Megan Devine: This book challenges societal expectations around grief and offers a compassionate approach to navigating loss. Megan Devine, a psychotherapist who experienced profound loss herself, provides practical advice and validation for those struggling with grief. This book emphasizes the importance of acknowledging and honouring one's unique grief journey.

Think about a woman who feels isolated in her grief might find solace in reading "It's OK That You're Not OK," gaining validation and practical tools for coping.

7. "When Breath Becomes Air" by Paul Kalanithi: In this memoir, neurosurgeon Paul Kalanithi reflects on his life and impending death after being diagnosed with terminal cancer. With eloquence and insight,

Kalanithi explores the meaning of life, death, and legacy. This book offers a profound perspective on facing mortality and the process of saying goodbye.

Imagine a person who loses a loved one to illness might find comfort in reading "When Breath Becomes Air," connecting with Kalanithi's reflections and finding meaning in their own experiences.

8. "The Grief Recovery Handbook" by John W. James and Russell Friedman: This practical guide offers a step-by-step approach to recovering from grief. The authors, both grief experts, provide tools and exercises for processing emotions, addressing unresolved issues, and finding a path towards healing. This book is designed to be a hands-on resource for those seeking support in their grief journey.

Think about a person who struggles with unresolved grief might use "The Grief Recovery Handbook" as a practical guide to navigate their emotions and find healing.

9. "Option B: Facing Adversity, Building Resilience, and Finding Joy" by Sheryl Sandberg and Adam Grant: In this book, Sheryl Sandberg shares her experiences of grief following the sudden death of her husband. Co-authored with psychologist Adam Grant, the book explores resilience, finding meaning, and building joy after loss. It offers practical advice and inspirational stories to help individuals navigate adversity.

Imagine a person who loses their spouse might find inspiration and practical tools in "Option B," gaining insights into resilience and finding moments of joy amidst their grief.

10. "Tuesdays with Morrie" by Mitch Albom: This memoir recounts the lessons learned from weekly conversations

between the author and his former college professor, Morrie Schwartz, who is dying from ALS. The book explores themes of life, death, and the importance of meaningful connections. It offers a heartwarming and philosophical perspective on facing mortality and finding meaning in life.

Think about a person who loses a mentor might find comfort in reading "Tuesdays with Morrie," connecting with the lessons and reflections shared in the book.

Books and literature can provide valuable support, comfort, and guidance for individuals navigating the complexities of grief. By exploring the experiences and insights of others, individuals can find validation, inspiration, and practical tools for coping with loss and finding a path towards healing and hope.

Websites and Online Tools

In the digital age, websites and online tools have become invaluable resources for individuals coping with grief. These platforms offer a wealth of information, support, and community connections, making them accessible options for those seeking guidance and comfort. Here are some recommended websites and online tools for navigating grief:

1. What's Your Grief (whatsyourgrief.com): This comprehensive website offers articles, podcasts, online courses, and other resources focused on various aspects of grief. Founded by mental health professionals, What's Your Grief provides practical advice, personal stories, and research-based information to help individuals navigate their grief journey.

Imagine a person who loses their partner might visit What's Your Grief to read articles about coping strategies and join online courses to learn more about managing their emotions.

2. Grief.com (grief.com): Created by grief expert David Kessler, Grief.com provides resources, support, and education on grief and loss. The website includes articles, videos, webinars, and a directory of support groups. David Kessler's work builds on the foundation laid by Elisabeth Kübler-Ross, offering insights into the five stages of grief and beyond.

Think about a woman who loses her child might visit Grief.com to watch webinars and connect with support groups to find comfort and understanding.

3. The Compassionate Friends (compassionatefriends.org): This organization provides support to families who have experienced the death of a child. The Compassionate Friends offers online communities, local chapter meetings, and resources for coping with grief. The website includes articles, personal stories, and information about upcoming events and support groups.

Imagine a family who loses their son might find support through The Compassionate Friends' online communities and local chapter meetings.

4. GriefShare (griefshare.org): GriefShare is a network of support groups for individuals grieving the loss of a loved one. The website offers information about local support groups, online resources, and a daily email encouragement program. GriefShare groups are

faith-based and provide a supportive environment for individuals to share their experiences and find comfort.

Think about a person who loses their spouse might join a local GriefShare group to connect with others and participate in the daily email program for ongoing support.

5. Modern Loss (modernloss.com): Modern Loss is an online community and resource hub that explores the complexities of grief in a candid and relatable way. The website features personal essays, advice columns, and interactive forums where individuals can share their stories and seek support. Modern Loss aims to break the stigma around grief and create a space for open conversation.

Imagine a young adult who loses their parent might find solace in reading personal essays on Modern Loss and connecting with others in the interactive forums.

6. Open to Hope (opentohope.com): Founded by Dr. Gloria Horsley and Dr. Heidi Horsley, Open to Hope provides resources and support for individuals experiencing grief. The website includes articles, podcasts, videos, and a community forum. Open to Hope aims to offer hope and inspiration to those navigating the difficult journey of grief.

Think about a person who loses their sibling might listen to podcasts on Open to Hope to hear from experts and others who have experienced similar losses.

7. Centre for Loss and Life Transition (centerforloss.com): Led by grief counsellor and author Dr. Alan Wolfelt, the Centre for Loss and Life Transition offers resources and

education on grief and mourning. The website includes articles, books, training programs, and a directory of grief counsellors. Dr. Wolfelt's work emphasizes the importance of acknowledging and honouring grief.

Imagine a woman who loses her mother might visit the Centre for Loss and Life Transition to read articles and find a grief counsellor for additional support.

8. Refuge in Grief (refugeingrief.com): Created by grief advocate Megan Devine, Refuge in Grief offers resources and support for individuals experiencing deep loss. The website includes articles, online courses, and a community forum. Megan Devine's approach focuses on validating the pain of grief and offering practical tools for coping.

Think about a man who loses his best friend might join an online course on Refuge in Grief to learn coping strategies and connect with others who understand his pain.

9. Dougy Centre (dougy.org): The Dougy Centre provides support for children, teens, and families grieving a death. The website includes resources, articles, and information about local programs and support groups. The Dougy Centre's work emphasizes the importance of addressing the unique needs of grieving children and teens.

Imagine a family who loses their father might access resources on the Dougy Centre website to help their children navigate their grief.

10. National Alliance for Grieving Children (childrengrieve.org): This organization offers resources and support for children, teens, and their families

experiencing grief. The website includes articles, toolkits, webinars, and a directory of support programs. The National Alliance for Grieving Children aims to raise awareness and provide comprehensive support for grieving children.

Think about a parent who loses their child might visit the National Alliance for Grieving Children website to find resources and support programs for their surviving children.

Websites and online tools provide valuable resources for individuals navigating the complexities of grief. By accessing these platforms, individuals can find information, support networks, and guidance to help them on their grief journey. These resources offer a sense of connection and hope, empowering individuals to find moments of healing and resilience.

Apps for Grief Support

In today's digital age, mobile apps have become a convenient and accessible tool for providing grief support. These apps offer various features, including guided meditations, journaling prompts, support communities, and resources for coping with loss. Here are some recommended apps for grief support:

1. GriefWorks: Developed by leading grief therapist Julia Samuel, GriefWorks offers a range of tools and resources to help individuals navigate their grief. The app includes guided meditations, mindfulness exercises, and stories from others who have experienced loss. It also offers a journal feature where users can record their thoughts and feelings.

Imagine a person who loses their sibling might use GriefWorks to practice guided meditations and keep a daily journal of their emotions.

2. MyGrief: MyGrief provides resources and support for individuals experiencing grief. The app includes articles, videos, and interactive tools to help users understand and process their grief. It also offers a diary feature for recording thoughts and reflections, as well as a community forum for connecting with others.

Think about a woman who lost her spouse who might use MyGrief to access educational resources and participate in the community forum for support.

3. Calm: While not specifically designed for grief, the Calm app offers a range of mindfulness and meditation practices that can be beneficial for managing grief-related stress and anxiety. The app includes guided meditations, sleep stories, and breathing exercises to promote relaxation and emotional well-being.

Imagine a person who loses their parent might use Calm to practice daily meditation and find moments of tranquillity amidst their grief.

4. Headspace: Similar to Calm, Headspace offers mindfulness and meditation practices that can help individuals cope with grief. The app includes guided meditations, mindfulness exercises, and sleep aids designed to reduce stress and improve emotional health. Headspace also offers specific meditations focused on grief and loss.

Think about a man who loses his best friend might use

Headspace to practice mindfulness exercises and find solace in guided meditations focused on grief.

5. Grief Support Network: This app provides access to a community of individuals experiencing grief, allowing users to share their stories and offer mutual support. The Grief Support Network app includes discussion forums, personal journaling features, and resources for understanding grief. It offers a safe space for users to connect with others who understand their pain.

Imagine a woman who loses her child might use the Grief Support Network app to connect with other bereaved parents and share her experiences in the discussion forums.

6. Wysa: Wysa is an AI-driven mental health app that offers emotional support and resources for coping with grief. The app includes guided exercises, mindfulness practices, and a chat feature where users can talk with Wysa, a friendly AI companion. Wysa also offers access to professional therapists for additional support.

Think about a person who feels overwhelmed by their grief might use Wysa to practice mindfulness exercises and chat with the AI companion for immediate support.

7. Mend: Originally designed for individuals recovering from breakups, Mend offers tools and resources that can also be beneficial for coping with grief. The app includes guided journaling, audio exercises, and self-care tips to promote emotional healing. Mend provides a structured program to help users navigate their grief journey.

Imagine a person who loses their partner might use Mend to follow the guided journaling prompts and practice self-care exercises.

8. Reflectly: Reflectly is a journaling app that uses AI to help users track their emotions and reflect on their experiences. The app offers daily prompts, mood tracking, and personalized insights to promote emotional well-being. Reflectly can be a valuable tool for individuals seeking to process their grief through journaling.

Think about a teenager who loses a friend might use Reflectly to record their thoughts and track their emotional progress over time.

9. Jour: Jour is a guided journaling app that provides prompts and exercises to help users explore their emotions and experiences. The app includes mindfulness practices, goal-setting features, and personalized insights to support emotional health. Jour can be particularly helpful for individuals seeking to process their grief through structured journaling.

Imagine a woman who loses her parent might use Jour to follow guided journaling exercises and reflect on her memories and emotions.

10. BetterHelp: BetterHelp offers online therapy with licensed therapists through video, phone, and text communication. The app provides a convenient and accessible way to receive professional support for grief and other mental health concerns. BetterHelp matches users with therapists based on their preferences and needs.

Think about a person who loses their sibling might use BetterHelp to connect with a grief therapist and receive ongoing support through video sessions.

Mobile apps for grief support provide accessible and convenient tools for managing the complexities of grief. By incorporating these apps into their daily routine, individuals can find practical resources, emotional support, and moments of peace and healing. These digital tools empower individuals to take an active role in their grief journey and find the support they need.

Coping with Holidays and Anniversaries

Holidays and anniversaries can be particularly challenging times for individuals grieving the loss of a loved one. These occasions often bring heightened emotions, memories, and a sense of longing for the presence of the deceased. Finding ways to navigate these difficult moments is essential for maintaining emotional well-being and honouring the memory of the loved one. Here are some strategies for coping with holidays and anniversaries:

1. Plan Ahead: Anticipating the emotional challenges of holidays and anniversaries can help you prepare and develop a plan for coping. Consider how you want to spend the day, who you want to be with, and what activities might bring you comfort. Having a plan in place can provide a sense of control and reduce anxiety.

Imagine a person who loses their partner might decide to spend their anniversary with close friends who understand their grief. They plan a small gathering where they can share memories and find comfort in their support.

2. Honor the Memory: Finding ways to honour the

memory of the loved one can provide a sense of connection and meaning. This might involve creating a special ritual, lighting a candle, visiting their gravesite, or participating in an activity that was meaningful to them. These acts of remembrance can offer comfort and a way to celebrate their life.

Think about a family who loses their mother might visit her favourite park on her birthday, spending time together and sharing stories about her. This ritual provides a sense of connection and helps keep her memory alive.

3. Allow Yourself to Feel: It's important to acknowledge and accept the full range of emotions that arise during holidays and anniversaries. Allow yourself to feel sadness, anger, joy, or any other emotions without judgment. Recognizing these feelings as a natural part of the grieving process can help you navigate them more effectively.

Imagine a person who loses their child might feel a mix of sorrow and gratitude during the holidays. By acknowledging these emotions and giving themselves permission to feel, they can find moments of peace and acceptance.

4. Create New Traditions: Establishing new traditions can help you navigate the absence of the loved one while creating a sense of continuity and connection. Consider incorporating activities that honour their memory or bring you joy. New traditions can provide a sense of renewal and help you move forward while still honouring the past.

Think about a couple who loses their son might start a new tradition of volunteering at a local charity on his birthday, giving back to the community in his honour. This new tradition provides a sense of purpose and fulfilment.

5. Seek Support: Surrounding yourself with supportive friends and family can provide comfort and encouragement during challenging times. Share your feelings and experiences with those who understand and care about you. Building a network of support can provide valuable resources and emotional strength.

Imagine a person who loses their spouse might lean on their close friends for support during the holidays, sharing their grief and finding comfort in their presence. These relationships provide a sense of community and understanding.

6. Practice Self-Care: Prioritizing self-care is essential during holidays and anniversaries. Engage in activities that bring you comfort and relaxation, such as taking a walk, practicing mindfulness, or enjoying a favourite hobby. Taking care of your physical and emotional well-being can help you navigate the heightened emotions of these occasions.

Think about a woman who loses her father might spend time in nature on his birthday, finding solace and tranquillity in the natural surroundings. This self-care practice helps her manage her emotions and find moments of peace.

7. Be Flexible: Recognize that your needs and emotions may change from year to year. Be open to adjusting

your plans and traditions as needed. Allow yourself the flexibility to do what feels right for you in the moment, whether that means participating in social activities or spending time alone.

Imagine a person who loses their sibling might choose to spend one anniversary quietly reflecting at home, while the next year they might participate in a family gathering. Being flexible with their approach helps them navigate their grief in a way that feels authentic and supportive.

8. Seek Professional Support: If you find the emotions of holidays and anniversaries overwhelming, consider seeking professional support from a therapist or grief counsellor. These professionals can provide tools and strategies for managing intense emotions and offer a safe space to explore your grief.

Think about a man who loses his mother might seek therapy to address the heightened emotions he feels during the holidays. The therapist provides him with coping strategies and support, helping him navigate these challenging times.

9. Connect with Others Who Understand: Participating in support groups or online communities can provide a sense of connection and understanding. Sharing your experiences with others who have experienced similar losses can offer validation and comfort. These connections can help you feel less alone in your grief.

Imagine a person who loses their partner might join an online support group for widows and widowers. Through the group, they connect with others who share their experiences and offer mutual support during difficult times.

10. Focus on the Positive: While it's natural to feel sadness and longing during holidays and anniversaries, try to also focus on positive memories and moments of joy. Reflecting on the happy times you shared with your loved one can provide comfort and a sense of gratitude. Balancing the sorrow with positive memories can help you navigate these challenging occasions.

Think about a family who loses their child might spend time sharing their favourite memories and looking through photo albums on their child's birthday. This focus on positive memories helps them celebrate their child's life and find moments of joy amidst their grief.

Coping with holidays and anniversaries while grieving can be a challenging and emotional experience. By planning ahead, honouring the memory of the loved one, seeking support, and practising self-care, individuals can navigate these difficult times and find moments of peace and healing. These strategies offer a path towards honouring the past while embracing the future with resilience and hope.

Professional Organizations and Support Services

Professional organizations and support services dedicated to grief and bereavement provide invaluable resources, education, and support for individuals navigating the complexities of loss. These organizations offer a range of services, including counselling, support groups, educational materials, and training for professionals. Here are some recommended professional organizations and support services for coping with grief:

1. National Hospice and Palliative Care Organization (NHPCO): NHPCO is a leading organization dedicated to hospice and palliative care. They provide resources and support for individuals and families facing terminal illness and grief. NHPCO offers educational materials, support groups, and a directory of hospice and palliative care providers.

Imagine a family coping with the impending loss of a loved one might access NHPCO resources to find a local hospice provider and receive guidance on end-of-life care and bereavement support.

2. American Counselling Association (ACA): The ACA is a professional organization that supports counsellors and mental health professionals. They provide resources, training, and publications on a wide range of topics, including grief and bereavement. The ACA also offers a directory of licensed counsellors who specialize in grief support.

Think about a person seeking professional counselling for grief might use the ACA directory to find a qualified therapist in their area.

3. Association for Death Education and Counselling (ADEC): ADEC is an interdisciplinary organization dedicated to promoting excellence in death education, care of the dying, grief counselling, and research in thanatology. They offer resources, publications, and training for professionals working in the field of grief and bereavement.

Imagine a grief counsellor might join ADEC to

access professional development opportunities and stay informed about the latest research and best practices in grief support.

4. National Alliance for Children's Grief (NACG): NACG provides resources and support for children, teens, and their families experiencing grief. They offer educational materials, training programs, and a directory of support services. NACG aims to raise awareness and provide comprehensive support for grieving children and their families.

Think about a parent seeking support for their grieving child might access NACG resources to find local programs and educational materials tailored to children's grief.

5. The Dougy Centre for Grieving Children and Families: The Dougy Centre is a leading organization providing support for children, teens, and families who are grieving a death. They offer peer support groups, educational resources, and training for professionals. The Dougy Centre's work emphasizes the importance of addressing the unique needs of grieving children and teens.

Imagine a family who loses a parent might participate in a peer support group at The Dougy Centre, finding comfort and connection with others who understand their grief.

6. Hospice Foundation of America (HFA): HFA provides support and education for individuals and families facing terminal illness, death, and grief. They offer webinars, publications, and a directory of hospice providers. HFA also organizes annual educational conferences on grief and bereavement.

Think about a caregiver seeking information on end-of-life care and bereavement might access HFA resources and attend a webinar on coping with grief.

7. National Suicide Prevention Lifeline: The National Suicide Prevention Lifeline offers immediate support for individuals experiencing suicidal thoughts or emotional distress. They provide crisis intervention, emotional support, and referrals to local services. The Lifeline is available 24/7 via phone and online chat.

Imagine a person feeling overwhelmed by their grief might contact the National Suicide Prevention Lifeline for immediate support and guidance.

8. Grief Recovery Institute: The Grief Recovery Institute offers educational programs, support services, and resources for individuals experiencing grief. Their Grief Recovery Method provides a structured approach to processing grief and finding healing. The Institute also offers certification programs for professionals seeking to specialize in grief support.

Consider a person struggling with unresolved grief might participate in a Grief Recovery Method program to find structured support and practical tools for healing.

9. Compassionate Friends: Compassionate Friends is an organization that provides support for families who have experienced the death of a child. They offer local chapter meetings, online communities, and resources for coping with grief. Compassionate Friends aims to provide a supportive environment for families navigating the profound loss of a child.

Imagine a family who loses their daughter might join a local Compassionate Friends chapter to connect with others who understand their grief and offer mutual support.

10. American Foundation for Suicide Prevention (AFSP): AFSP is dedicated to saving lives and bringing hope to those affected by suicide. They provide resources, support groups, and educational programs for individuals and families affected by suicide loss. AFSP also funds research and advocacy efforts to prevent suicide and improve mental health support.

Think about a person who loses a loved one to suicide might access AFSP resources to find a support group and participate in educational programs on coping with suicide loss.

Professional organizations and support services play a crucial role in providing resources, education, and support for individuals experiencing grief. By accessing these services, individuals can find the tools, guidance, and community connections needed to navigate their grief journey and find moments of healing and hope.

CHAPTER 14: PRACTICAL TIPS FOR SUPPORTING SOMEONE GRIEVING

Understanding the Grieving Process

Supporting someone who is grieving can be challenging, as each person's experience with grief is unique. Understanding the grieving process and how to provide compassionate support can make a significant difference in the lives of those who are mourning. Here are some practical tips for supporting someone who is grieving:

1. Be Present: One of the most important ways to support someone who is grieving is to simply be present. Offer your time and companionship and let them know you are there for them. Sometimes, just sitting quietly with someone can provide immense comfort.

You might spend an afternoon with a grieving friend, listening to their memories and sharing moments of silence. Your presence can provide a sense of connection and support.

2. Listen Without Judgment: Allow the grieving person to express their emotions and thoughts without judgment. Grief can bring up a wide range of emotions, including anger, guilt, sadness, and confusion. Offer a listening ear and validate their feelings, letting them know it's okay to feel however they feel.

A grieving family member might share feelings of anger and regret. By listening without judgment and acknowledging their emotions, you provide a safe space for them to express themselves.

3. Offer Practical Help: Grieving individuals may struggle with daily tasks and responsibilities. Offer practical help, such as preparing meals, running errands, or assisting with household chores. These acts of kindness can alleviate some of the burden and show your support.

Offering to cook dinner for a grieving friend or help them with grocery shopping. These practical gestures can provide much-needed relief during a difficult time.

4. Respect Their Process: Each person's grieving process is unique, and there is no "right" way to grieve. Respect their individual journey and avoid imposing your own expectations or timelines. Allow them to grieve at their own pace and in their own way.

A grieving colleague might need more time off work than you expected. Respect their need for time and space and offer support when they are ready to return.

5. Avoid Clichés and Platitudes: While well-intentioned,

clichés and platitudes can sometimes minimize the grieving person's experience. Avoid phrases like "Everything happens for a reason" or "They're in a better place now." Instead, offer genuine empathy and understanding.

Imagine, instead of saying, "You'll get over it soon," you can say, "I can't imagine how hard this must be for you. I'm here for you."

6. Encourage Professional Support: Grieving individuals may benefit from professional support, such as therapy or counselling. Gently encourage them to seek help if they are struggling to cope. Offer to help them find resources or accompany them to appointments if needed.

Think about you might suggest, "It might be helpful to talk to a counsellor about what you're going through. I can help you find someone if you'd like."

7. Share Memories and Stories: Sharing memories and stories about the deceased can provide comfort and help keep their memory alive. Encourage the grieving person to talk about their loved one and share your own memories as well.

Consider saying something like, "I remember when your dad used to tell those funny stories at family gatherings. He had such a great sense of humour."

8. Be Patient: Grief is a long and often unpredictable journey. Be patient and understanding, recognizing that the grieving process can take time and may involve ups and downs. Offer ongoing support and let them know you are there for the long haul.

Think about you might check in regularly with a grieving friend, offering a listening ear and companionship even months after the loss.

9. Respect Their Privacy: While it's important to offer support, also respect their need for privacy and space. Allow them to take the time they need to process their emotions and reach out when they are ready.

You can say, "I understand if you need some time alone. I'm here whenever you want to talk or need anything."

10. Offer Continued Support: Grief does not have a set timeline, and the need for support may continue long after the initial loss. Continue to offer your support and check in with the grieving person regularly, especially during significant dates and anniversaries.

Send a thoughtful message or visit a grieving friend on the anniversary of their loved one's passing, letting them know you are thinking of them.

Supporting someone who is grieving requires empathy, patience, and a willingness to be present. By offering compassionate and practical support, you can help them navigate their grief journey and find moments of healing and hope.

Communication Tips for Supporting Grievers

Effective communication is key to providing meaningful support for someone who is grieving. Knowing what to say—and what not to say—can make a significant difference in their healing process. Here are some communication tips for supporting grievers:

1. Use Empathetic Language: Use language that conveys empathy and understanding. Acknowledge their pain and let them know you are there to support them. Phrases like "I'm so sorry for your loss" or "I'm here for you" can provide comfort and show that you care.

Saying "I can't imagine how difficult this must be for you. Please know that I'm here to support you in any way I can."

2. Validate Their Feelings: Grief can bring up a wide range of emotions, and it's important to validate their feelings without judgment. Let them know that it's okay to feel however they feel, whether it's sadness, anger, guilt, or confusion.

You can say, "It's completely normal to feel this way. Your feelings are valid, and it's okay to express them."

3. Avoid Minimizing Statements: Avoid statements that minimize their grief or suggest that they should "move on" or "be strong." These statements can be hurtful and dismissive of their emotions. Instead, offer genuine support and understanding.

Instead of saying, "At least they're in a better place," you might say, "I'm so sorry for your loss. It's okay to feel whatever you're feeling."

4. Be a Good Listener: Sometimes, the best way to support someone who is grieving is to simply listen. Allow them to share their thoughts and feelings without interrupting or offering unsolicited advice. Listening with empathy and without judgment can provide immense comfort.

Saying "I'm here to listen if you want to talk about it. You don't have to go through this alone."

5. Offer Specific Help: Instead of saying, "Let me know if you need anything," offer specific ways you can help. This can make it easier for them to accept support and feel less overwhelmed by the burden of asking for help.

Imagine you might say, "I can help with grocery shopping or take care of the kids for a few hours if you need some time for yourself."

6. Respect Their Boundaries: Respect their need for privacy and space. Avoid pressing them to talk or share more than they are comfortable with. Let them know that it's okay to take their time and reach out when they are ready.

For example, you might say, "I understand if you don't want to talk right now. I'm here whenever you feel ready to share or need some company."

7. Use Their Loved One's Name: Using the deceased person's name can show that you remember and honour their memory. It can also encourage the grieving person to share memories and feel that their loved one is still being acknowledged.

Say "I remember when Sarah used to bake those amazing cookies. She had such a warm and generous spirit."

8. Be Mindful of Cultural Differences: Different cultures have varying practices and beliefs around grief and mourning. Be mindful of these differences and respect their cultural practices and traditions. This can help you provide more meaningful and culturally sensitive support.

You might ask, "Is there anything specific from your cultural traditions that I can help with or support during this time?"

9. Avoid Giving Unsolicited Advice: While it's natural to want to offer solutions, avoid giving unsolicited advice unless they specifically ask for it. Instead, focus on providing emotional support and being a compassionate presence.

Imagine instead of saying, "You should try to get out more," you might say, "I'm here to support you in whatever way feels right for you."

10. Offer Ongoing Support: Grief does not have a set timeline, and the need for support may continue long after the initial loss. Continue to offer your support and check in regularly, especially during significant dates and anniversaries.

Think about you might send a thoughtful message or visit a grieving friend on the anniversary of their loved one's passing, letting them know you are thinking of them.

Effective communication is essential for providing meaningful support to someone who is grieving. By using empathetic language, validating their feelings, and being a good listener, you can help them navigate their grief journey and find moments of healing and hope.

Self-Care Tips for Caregivers

Supporting someone who is grieving can be emotionally taxing, and caregivers need to practice self-care to maintain their own well-being. Taking care of yourself allows you to provide better support for others and ensures that you do not become overwhelmed or burnt out. Here are some self-care tips for caregivers:

1. Set Boundaries: Establish clear boundaries to protect your own emotional and physical well-being. It's important to know your limits and communicate them effectively. This might involve setting aside specific times for self-care and ensuring that you have personal space when needed.

Something like "I can help you with errands this afternoon, but I need some time for myself in the evening to recharge."

2. Practice Mindfulness: Mindfulness practices, such as meditation and deep breathing, can help you stay grounded and manage stress. Take a few moments each day to focus on your breath, observe your thoughts without judgment, and practice being present in the moment.

Think of spending 10 minutes each morning practising deep breathing exercises to start your day with a sense of calm and clarity.

3. Seek Support: Caregivers also need support. Reach out to friends, family, or support groups to share your experiences and receive emotional support. Talking to others who understand your role can provide validation and comfort.

Join a support group for caregivers to connect with others who are also providing support for grieving individuals.

4. Prioritize Self-Care Activities: Engage in activities that

bring you joy and relaxation. This might include hobbies, exercise, spending time in nature, or simply taking a break to read a book or watch a movie. Prioritizing self-care helps replenish your energy and maintain your well-being.

Think about scheduling regular walks in the park or setting aside time each week to pursue a hobby you enjoy.

5. Get Enough Rest: Ensuring that you get enough sleep is crucial for maintaining your physical and emotional health. Create a relaxing bedtime routine, avoid screens before bed, and prioritize getting enough rest each night.

Establishing a bedtime routine that includes reading a book or listening to calming music to help you unwind and prepare for sleep.

6. Eat Nutritious Foods: Maintaining a healthy diet can help you manage stress and maintain your energy levels. Aim to eat a balanced diet that includes plenty of fruits, vegetables, whole grains, and lean proteins. Avoid excessive caffeine and sugar, which can contribute to stress and fatigue.

Prepare nutritious meals ahead of time and keep healthy snacks on hand to ensure you are nourishing your body.

7. Exercise Regularly: Regular physical activity can help reduce stress, improve mood, and boost overall well-being. Find an exercise routine that you enjoy and can maintain consistently, whether it's walking, yoga, swimming, or another form of exercise.

Incorporate a daily walk or a weekly yoga class into your routine to help manage stress and improve your physical health.

8. Practice Self-Compassion: Be kind to yourself and recognize that caregiving can be challenging. Allow yourself to feel and process your emotions without judgment. Practice self-compassion by acknowledging your efforts and treating yourself with the same kindness you would offer to a friend.

Remind yourself, "I'm doing my best, and it's okay to take a break when I need it."

9. Stay Connected: Maintain connections with friends and family who can provide support and companionship. Social connections are important for emotional well-being and can provide a sense of community and belonging.

Schedule regular phone calls or meetups with friends to stay connected and receive emotional support.

10. Seek Professional Help: If you find yourself feeling overwhelmed, anxious, or depressed, consider seeking professional help. A therapist or counsellor can provide support and guidance, helping you navigate the challenges of caregiving and maintain your well-being.

Schedule regular therapy sessions to discuss your experiences and receive professional support.

Practising self-care is essential for caregivers to maintain their own well-being and provide meaningful support to others. By setting boundaries, seeking support, and prioritizing self-care activities, caregivers can navigate the challenges of caregiving and find moments of healing and hope.

CHAPTER 15: MORE PRACTICAL TIPS

Helping Children Cope with Grief

Children process grief differently than adults, and their understanding of death and loss evolves as they grow. Supporting a grieving child requires sensitivity, patience, and clear communication. Here are some practical tips for helping children cope with grief:

1. Use Simple and Clear Language: When explaining death to children, use simple, clear, and age-appropriate language. Avoid euphemisms that can confuse them, such as "passed away" or "gone to sleep." Instead, use direct terms like "died" to help them understand the concept of death.

Imagine saying "Grandma died, which means her body stopped working and she can't be with us anymore."

2. Encourage Questions: Children may have many questions about death and what it means. Encourage them to ask questions and answer them as honestly as possible. It's okay to admit if you don't have all the answers and to explore their thoughts and feelings together.

Think about a child might ask, "Will we see Grandma again?" You could respond, "We won't see her in the same way, but we can keep her memory alive by talking about her and remembering the happy times we shared."

3. Provide Reassurance: Reassure children that their feelings are normal and that it's okay to feel sad, angry, or confused. Let them know that they are safe and that it's okay to express their emotions in healthy ways.

"It's okay to feel sad and cry. I'm here with you, and we can talk about how you're feeling whenever you want."

4. Maintain Routines: Keeping a sense of routine and normalcy can provide comfort and stability for grieving children. Maintain regular daily activities, such as mealtimes, bedtime routines, and school schedules, to help them feel secure.

5. Use Books and Stories: Reading books about loss and grief can help children understand their emotions and the grieving process. Choose age-appropriate books that address death and loss in a gentle and relatable way.

6. Encourage Expression Through Play: Children often express their emotions through play. Provide opportunities for them to engage in creative activities, such as drawing, painting, or playing with dolls or action figures. These activities can help them process their feelings in a safe and supportive environment.

Think about how you might set up an art station with crayons and paper, encouraging the child to draw pictures that express their feelings.

7. Create Rituals and Memories: Help children create

rituals and memories to honour their loved one. This might include making a memory box, planting a tree, or creating a scrapbook with photos and mementoes. These activities can provide a sense of connection and help keep the loved one's memory alive.

Imagine how you might work with the child to create a memory box filled with special items that remind them of their loved one.

8. Be Patient and Understanding: Grieving children may experience a range of emotions and behaviours, including regression, clinginess, or acting out. Be patient and understanding, recognizing that these behaviours are a normal part of the grieving process.

Think about a child who might become clingier or have trouble sleeping. Offer comfort and reassurance, letting them know that you are there for them.

9. Seek Professional Support: If a child is struggling to cope with their grief, consider seeking support from a therapist or counsellor who specializes in working with children. Professional support can provide additional tools and strategies to help the child navigate their emotions.

10. Model Healthy Coping: Children often look to adults for cues on how to handle difficult situations. Model healthy coping strategies, such as talking about your feelings, seeking support, and practising self-care. This can help children learn to navigate their own grief in healthy ways.

Consider something like "I'm feeling sad today because I miss Grandpa. I'm going to take a walk to help me feel better. Would you like to come with me?"

Supporting a grieving child requires sensitivity, patience, and clear communication. By using simple language, encouraging expression, and providing reassurance, you can help children navigate their grief and find moments of healing and hope.

CHAPTER 16: STORIES OF OVERCOMING GRIEF

Raj's Resilience

Raj stood at the edge of the riverbank, the place where he and his father had spent countless hours fishing, talking, and dreaming about the future. It had been two years since his father's passing, and the pain of his loss still felt raw and overwhelming. Raj's journey through grief had been marked by deep sorrow, but also moments of connection, resilience, and growth.

In the immediate aftermath of his father's death, Raj felt as though his world had come to a standstill. The routines and rituals they had shared, such as their weekend fishing trips and long conversations, now felt empty and meaningless. The riverbank, once a place of joy and camaraderie, now seemed like a stark reminder of his absence. Raj struggled to find his footing, feeling lost and disconnected from the world around him.

Recognizing the need for support, Raj reached out to a grief counsellor. In the safe space of his counsellor's office, Raj began to explore the depths of his sorrow. His counsellor introduced him to mindfulness and meditation, practices that helped him stay present and manage his overwhelming emotions. Through therapy, Raj learned to navigate the complexities of his grief and develop healthy coping strategies.

One of the most significant steps in Raj's healing journey was creating rituals to honour his father's memory. Each weekend, he would visit the riverbank, bringing along his father's favourite fishing rod. He would sit quietly by the water, reflecting on their time together and the memories they had shared. This ritual provided a structured time for Raj to connect with his emotions and honour his father's legacy. The serene surroundings of the riverbank brought him a sense of peace and connection.

Raj also found solace in creative expression. He began to write letters to his father, expressing his thoughts and feelings. These letters became a cherished collection, a testament to their bond and his journey through grief. Writing allowed Raj to process his emotions in a tangible and meaningful way, providing a sense of release and connection.

To further honour his father's memory, Raj decided to volunteer at a local community centre where his father had been an active member. His father had always been passionate about helping others, and Raj wanted to continue his legacy of kindness and generosity. He spent his weekends organizing community events and fundraisers, channelling his grief into positive action.

Volunteering became a living tribute to his father's spirit and brought joy and connection to Raj's life.

As he continued to heal, Raj set new goals for himself. He decided to pursue further education, enrolling in courses that aligned with his passion for environmental science. Inspired by his father's love for nature and the environment, Raj focused on sustainability and conservation. This pursuit provided a sense of purpose and fulfilment, allowing Raj to channel his grief into positive action.

Maintaining connections with friends and family was also crucial for Raj's recovery. He communicated his needs openly, allowing his loved ones to understand how to best support him. These relationships provided ongoing support and encouragement, helping Raj navigate the ups and downs of his grief. Sharing stories and memories of his father with friends and family created a sense of continuity and kept his spirit alive.

Raj also sought connection with others who understood his pain. He joined a support group for adults who had lost parents, where he found a community of individuals who shared similar experiences. The group provided a space for Raj to share his story and connect with others who validated his grief. These connections offered comfort and understanding, helping Raj feel less alone in his journey.

Through these small but significant steps, Raj found a path towards healing. He learned to live with his grief, understanding that it was a part of him but not all of him. He embraced the support of his loved ones, found fulfilment in creative expression and volunteering, and created new traditions that honoured his father's memory.

Raj's journey through grief is a testament to the power of resilience, support, and self-discovery. His story illustrates that while the pain of loss may never completely disappear, it is possible to find hope, meaning, and a renewed sense of purpose. By taking small steps towards healing and embracing new opportunities, Raj transformed his grief into a source of strength and continued to live a life filled with love and fulfilment.

Fatima's Recovery

Fatima stood in her garden, surrounded by the vibrant colours of the flowers she had planted in memory of her mother. Each bloom represented a cherished memory, a piece of the bond they had shared. It had been three years since her mother's passing, and while the pain of her loss still lingered, Fatima had found ways to honour her mother's legacy and navigate her grief with resilience and grace.

In the weeks following her mother's death, Fatima felt overwhelmed by a profound sense of emptiness. Her mother had been a guiding light in her life, a source of unwavering love and support. The routines they had shared—morning tea in the garden, weekend baking sessions, and late-night conversations—now felt hollow and devoid of joy. Fatima struggled to find a sense of purpose and direction without her mother's presence.

Seeking support, Fatima joined a grief support group. In the company of others who had experienced similar losses, she found a safe space to express her emotions and share her story. The group meetings provided a sense of camaraderie and understanding, reminding her that she was not alone in her grief. Through these connections, Fatima began to find solace and strength.

One of the most healing aspects of Fatima's journey was embracing her mother's love for gardening. Her mother had been an avid gardener, finding joy and peace in nurturing plants and flowers. To honour her memory, Fatima decided to transform her own garden into a tribute to her mother. She spent countless hours tending to the soil, planting her mother's favourite flowers, and creating a sanctuary of beauty and tranquillity.

The act of gardening became a therapeutic ritual for Fatima. Each bloom that flourished under her care was a reminder of her mother's enduring presence. The garden provided a space for reflection and connection, allowing Fatima to feel close to her mother even in her absence. The physical labour of gardening also helped Fatima channel her grief into positive action, providing a sense of accomplishment and purpose.

Fatima also found comfort in creative expression. She began to write poetry, capturing her emotions and memories in verse. Her poems became a poignant testament to her mother's impact on her life and a way to process her grief. Writing allowed Fatima to explore the depths of her sorrow and find moments of clarity and peace. Her poetry became a cherished collection, a tribute to her mother's legacy of love and resilience.

To further honour her mother's memory, Fatima decided to volunteer at a local community centre that offered gardening programs for children. Her mother had always believed in the power of community and the importance of giving back. By teaching children about gardening and sharing her passion, Fatima felt she was continuing her mother's work and spreading her spirit of generosity and kindness.

As she continued to heal, Fatima set new goals for herself. She decided to pursue a degree in horticulture, combining her love for gardening with her desire to honour her mother's legacy. The academic pursuit provided a sense of direction and fulfilment, allowing Fatima to channel her grief into a meaningful career. She found joy in learning and a renewed sense of purpose in her studies.

Maintaining connections with friends and family was also crucial for Fatima's recovery. She communicated openly about her grief, allowing her loved ones to understand her needs and offer support. These relationships provided a foundation of love and encouragement, helping Fatima navigate the ups and downs of her healing journey. Sharing stories and memories of her mother with friends and family kept her spirit alive and created a sense of continuity.

Fatima also sought connection with others who understood her pain. She joined an online support group for individuals who had lost parents, finding a virtual community of understanding and empathy. The group provided a space for Fatima to share her experiences and connect with others who validated her grief. These connections offered comfort and a sense of belonging, helping Fatima feel less alone in her journey.

Through these small but significant steps, Fatima found a path towards healing. She learned to live with her grief, understanding that it was a part of her but not all of her. She embraced the support of her loved ones, found fulfilment in creative expression and community service, and created new traditions that honoured her mother's memory.

Fatima's journey through grief is a testament to the power of resilience, support, and self-discovery. Her story illustrates that while the pain of loss may never completely disappear, it is possible to find hope, meaning, and a renewed sense of purpose. By taking small steps towards healing and embracing new opportunities, Fatima transformed her grief into a source of strength and continued to live a life filled with love and fulfilment.

CHAPTER 17: FINDING HOPE AFTER LOSS

Embracing Change

Finding hope after loss involves embracing change and discovering new paths forward. While the pain of loss may never completely disappear, it is possible to find moments of joy, meaning, and connection. Embracing change can be a powerful step towards healing and renewal.

1. Accepting the Reality of Loss: The first step towards embracing change is accepting the reality of the loss. This means acknowledging that life has changed and allowing yourself to grieve. Acceptance does not mean forgetting; it means recognizing the new reality and finding ways to move forward.

A wife who loses her husband might begin to accept the reality of his absence, allowing herself to grieve while finding ways to honour his memory.

2. Creating New Traditions: Establishing new traditions can help provide a sense of continuity and create

new memories. These traditions can be simple but meaningful, offering a way to honour the past while embracing the future.

A family might start a new tradition of gathering for a special meal on the anniversary of their loved one's passing, creating a new way to remember and celebrate their life.

3. Finding New Sources of Joy: Seek out new activities and experiences that bring joy and fulfilment. This might include hobbies, travel, or exploring new interests. Finding new sources of joy can help create positive experiences and provide a sense of purpose.

The chap who loses his partner might take up hiking, finding solace and joy in nature and physical activity.

4. Building a Supportive Community: Surround yourself with supportive friends, family, and community members who can provide comfort and understanding. Building a network of support can help you navigate the changes and challenges of life after loss.

The mum grieving her child might join a community group or club, finding new connections and support among like-minded individuals.

5. Setting New Goals: Setting new goals can provide a sense of direction and purpose. These goals can be personal, professional, or related to honouring the memory of the loved one. Working towards new goals can help create a sense of accomplishment and forward momentum.

A father who loses his daughter might set a goal to

complete a marathon in her honour, channelling his grief into a positive and meaningful challenge.

6. Embracing Personal Growth: Embrace the opportunities for personal growth that come with change. This might include developing new skills, pursuing education, or exploring new aspects of your identity. Personal growth can provide a sense of empowerment and renewal.

A daughter who loses her mother might decide to take a cooking class, developing a new skill and finding joy in an activity her mother loved.

7. Practicing Mindfulness: Mindfulness practices, such as meditation and deep breathing, can help you stay present and manage the overwhelming emotions of grief. These practices encourage you to observe your thoughts and feelings without judgment, providing a sense of calm and clarity.

A husband grieving his spouse might incorporate daily meditation into his routine, helping him find moments of peace and grounding.

8. Honouring the Memory: Finding ways to honour the memory of your loved one can provide a sense of connection and purpose. This might include creating a tribute, engaging in activities they enjoyed, or supporting causes they cared about.

Think about the sister who loses her brother and might participate in volunteer work for a charity he supported, keeping his memory alive through acts of service.

9. Allowing Yourself to Feel: Allow yourself to feel and

express your emotions, whether they are sadness, joy, anger, or hope. Embracing the full range of emotions is an important part of the healing process and helps you navigate the changes in your life.

A mother grieving her son might find herself laughing at a cherished memory one day and crying the next. Allowing herself to experience these emotions without judgment can support her healing.

10. Finding Meaning: Finding meaning in the experience of loss can provide a sense of purpose and direction. This might involve reflecting on the lessons learned, the impact of the loved one's life, and how their memory can inspire positive change.

The friend who loses his friend might find meaning in their shared experiences and use those memories to inspire personal growth and new endeavours.

Embracing change after loss is a journey that involves navigating a complex landscape of emotions and experiences. By accepting the reality of the loss, finding new sources of joy, and building a supportive community, it is possible to find moments of hope and renewal. Through mindfulness, personal growth, and honouring the memory of the loved one, you can navigate your grief journey and find a path towards healing and fulfilment.

Long-Term Strategies

Long-term strategies for coping with grief are essential for maintaining emotional well-being and finding a sense of balance and purpose. These strategies provide ongoing support and help individuals navigate the evolving landscape of grief.

1. Continuing Support Networks: Maintaining connections with support groups, friends, and family can provide ongoing emotional support. These networks offer a space to share experiences, receive validation, and find comfort.

The woman grieving her husband might continue attending a support group for widows, finding solace in the shared experiences and mutual support.

2. Ongoing Self-Care: Prioritize self-care activities that promote relaxation, well-being, and emotional balance. This might include regular exercise, meditation, hobbies, and spending time in nature. Consistent self-care practices help manage stress and support emotional health.

The father grieving his daughter might establish a daily routine that includes yoga and meditation, providing moments of peace and grounding.

3. Engaging in Meaningful Activities: Continue to engage in activities that bring joy, fulfilment, and a sense of purpose. These activities can provide a positive outlet for emotions and create new memories and experiences.

The father who loses his son might volunteer at a youth organization, finding joy and purpose in helping others.

4. Reflecting on Personal Growth: Periodically reflect on personal growth and how the grief journey has influenced your life. Acknowledge the progress made and the lessons learned and consider how these experiences have shaped your values and goals.

The daughter who loses her mother might journal about

her journey, reflecting on how her grief has inspired personal growth and new perspectives.

5. Creating a Legacy: Find ways to create a lasting legacy for the loved one, whether through charitable work, creative expression, or other meaningful activities. A legacy provides a sense of connection and purpose, honouring the memory of the loved one.

A family who loses their son might establish a scholarship fund in his name, supporting students and creating a lasting impact.

6. Seeking Professional Help: Consider ongoing professional support, such as therapy or counselling, to navigate the long-term impact of grief. Therapists can provide tools and strategies to help manage emotions and maintain emotional health.

A husband grieving his partner might continue seeing a therapist to explore his feelings and develop healthy coping mechanisms.

7. Embracing Change: Embrace the changes that come with the grief journey and find ways to adapt and grow. This might involve exploring new interests, developing new skills, or pursuing new opportunities. Embracing change can provide a sense of empowerment and renewal.

A daughter who loses her father might take up photography, finding a new passion and a way to capture and honour memories.

8. Finding Moments of Joy: Allow yourself to experience moments of joy and happiness, even amidst ongoing

grief. Finding joy in everyday experiences and new opportunities can provide a sense of balance and hope.

A mother grieving her child might find joy in spending time with friends, exploring new hobbies, and creating new memories.

9.   Practicing Mindfulness: Continue to practice mindfulness and meditation to stay present and manage emotions. These practices encourage you to observe your thoughts and feelings without judgment, providing a sense of calm and clarity.

The man grieving his wife might incorporate mindfulness practices into his daily routine, helping him find moments of peace and grounding.

10. Honouring the Memory: Continue to find ways to honour the memory of the loved one. This might include celebrating their life on significant dates, participating in activities they enjoyed, or supporting causes they cared about.

A family who loses their daughter might celebrate her birthday each year by participating in a charity run, honouring her memory through positive action.

Long-term strategies for coping with grief provide ongoing support and help individuals navigate the evolving landscape of their emotions and experiences. By maintaining support networks, engaging in meaningful activities, and embracing personal growth, it is possible to find a sense of balance and fulfilment. Through self-care, mindfulness, and honouring the memory of the loved one, you can continue to navigate your grief journey and find moments of healing and hope.

Moving Forward with Hope

Navigating the journey of grief is a profound and deeply personal experience. While the pain of loss may never completely disappear, it is possible to find moments of hope, healing, and renewal. By embracing the support of loved ones, engaging in meaningful activities, and honouring the memory of the loved one, individuals can find a path towards healing and a renewed sense of purpose.

1. Embracing Support: Surround yourself with supportive friends, family, and community members who can provide comfort and understanding. Seeking professional help, joining support groups, and accessing online resources can also provide valuable support and guidance.

2. Engaging in Meaningful Activities: Find activities that bring joy, fulfilment, and a sense of purpose. This might include hobbies, volunteer work, or creative expression. Engaging in meaningful activities can provide positive experiences and create new memories.

3. Honouring the Memory: Creating rituals and traditions to honour the memory of the loved one can provide comfort and a sense of connection. These might include celebrating significant dates, creating a memorial, or supporting causes they cared about.

4. Practicing Self-Care: Prioritize self-care activities that promote relaxation, well-being, and emotional balance. This might include regular exercise, meditation, hobbies, and spending time in nature. Consistent self-care practices help manage stress and support emotional

health.

5. Finding Moments of Joy: Allow yourself to experience moments of joy and happiness, even amidst ongoing grief. Finding joy in everyday experiences and new opportunities can provide a sense of balance and hope.

6. Seeking Professional Help: Consider ongoing professional support, such as therapy or counselling, to navigate the long-term impact of grief. Therapists can provide tools and strategies to help manage emotions and maintain emotional health.

7. Embracing Change: Embrace the changes that come with the grief journey and find ways to adapt and grow. This might involve exploring new interests, developing new skills, or pursuing new opportunities. Embracing change can provide a sense of empowerment and renewal.

8. Practicing Mindfulness: Continue to practice mindfulness and meditation to stay present and manage emotions. These practices encourage you to observe your thoughts and feelings without judgment, providing a sense of calm and clarity.

9. Reflecting on Personal Growth: Periodically reflect on personal growth and the ways in which the grief journey has influenced your life. Acknowledge the progress made and the lessons learned and consider how these experiences have shaped your values and goals.

10. Finding Meaning: Finding meaning in the experience of loss can provide a sense of purpose and direction. This might involve reflecting on the lessons learned, the impact of the loved one's life, and how their memory can

inspire positive change.

Moving forward with hope after loss involves embracing the support of loved ones, engaging in meaningful activities, and honouring the memory of the loved one. Through self-care, mindfulness, and personal growth, it is possible to navigate the grief journey and find moments of healing and renewal. By finding meaning in the experience of loss, individuals can create a legacy of love and resilience, honouring the memory of their loved one.

Let us carry forward this journey of love and compassion.

BEYOND TEARS

In the silence of the night, a whisper calls,
A gentle voice that echoes through the halls.
It speaks of love that never fades away,
And memories that in our hearts will stay.

We walked together, hand in trembling hand,
Through shadows cast upon this barren land.
Your laughter now a distant, cherished song,
A melody that in my soul belongs.

Beyond the tears that flow like endless streams,
Beyond the heartache shattering my dreams,
I find you in the stillness of the dawn,
In every breath, though you are gone.

Your essence lingers in the air I breathe,
A soothing balm upon the wounds that seethe.
In every star that lights the evening sky,
I see your face and wipe the tears I cry.

Grief is a river, wide and deep and cold,
It carries sorrow that no heart can hold.
Yet in its currents, something pure remains,
A testament to love that never wanes.

Through every storm, a rainbow finds its way,
Through every night, there comes a brighter day.
And though the pain may never truly cease,

There lies within the depths a quiet peace.

For love transcends the boundaries of time,
A sacred bond, eternal and sublime.
Beyond the tears, a tender light appears,
A beacon guiding through the darkest fears.

In every whispered breeze, your spirit speaks,
In every rustling leaf, the comfort seeks.
You are the strength that lifts me when I fall,
The silent answer to my anguished call.

So as I close this chapter, bittersweet,
I honour you in every heartbeat.
For grief and love are woven into one,
And through it all, our journey is not done.

Beyond the tears, there lies a brighter shore,
Where love endures and we shall part no more.
Until that day, I hold you close and dear,
Beyond the tears, forever you are near.

EPILOGUE

As you reach the end of "Beyond Tears: Navigating the Journey of Grief," take a moment to reflect on the path you have travelled through these pages. This book was crafted with the hope that it would provide you with comfort, understanding, and practical guidance as you navigate the complex and often painful journey of grief.

Grief is a deeply personal experience, unique to each individual, and yet it is a journey that we all share in some form. Through the stories, insights, and resources provided in this book, it is my hope that you have found a sense of connection and reassurance that you are not alone in your sorrow.

The process of healing from loss is not a linear path but a series of steps that ebb and flow with time. Some days may feel lighter, filled with moments of joy and remembrance, while others may be heavy with sadness and longing. This is the nature of grief, and it is important to honour your feelings and allow yourself the time and space to heal.

The personal stories shared within these pages are a testament to the resilience of the human spirit. They illustrate that while the pain of loss may never completely fade, it is possible to find a new normal, to build a life that honours the memory of your loved one, and to find moments of joy and purpose once more.

Remember that it is okay to seek support, whether through friends, family, support groups, or professional counselling. Reaching out for help is a sign of strength, not weakness. Surround yourself with those who understand and can offer you the empathy and support you need.

As you continue your journey beyond this book, carry with you the lessons and insights you have gained. Allow them to guide you, to provide you with comfort in moments of despair, and to remind you that healing is possible. Embrace the memories of your loved one, for they are a part of you and always will be.

May you find peace in the knowledge that you are walking this path with countless others who share in the experience of grief. Together, we can find strength, hope, and a renewed sense of purpose.

Thank you for allowing me to be a part of your journey. May "Beyond Tears" continue to be a source of light and comfort as you navigate the days ahead.

With compassion and understanding,

Dr Bhaskar Bora

REFERENCES

Recommended Reading and Resources

Books:
1. "On Grief and Grieving" by Elisabeth Kübler-Ross and David Kessler
2. "The Year of Magical Thinking" by Joan Didion
3. "Grief Counselling and Grief Therapy" by J. William Worden
4. "Healing After Loss: Daily Meditations for Working Through Grief" by Martha Whitmore Hickman
5. "A Grief Observed" by C.S. Lewis
6. "It's OK That You're Not OK: Meeting Grief and Loss in a Culture That Doesn't Understand" by Megan Devine
7. "When Breath Becomes Air" by Paul Kalanithi
8. "The Grief Recovery Handbook" by John W. James and Russell Friedman
9. "Option B: Facing Adversity, Building Resilience, and Finding Joy" by Sheryl Sandberg and Adam Grant
10. "Tuesdays with Morrie" by Mitch Albom

Websites:
1. What's Your Grief (whatsyourgrief.com)
2. Grief.com (grief.com)
3. The Compassionate Friends (compassionatefriends.org)
4. GriefShare (griefshare.org)

5. Modern Loss (modernloss.com)
6. Open to Hope (opentohope.com)
7. Centre for Loss and Life Transition (centerforloss.com)
8. Refuge in Grief (refugeingrief.com)
9. Dougy Centre (dougy.org)
10. National Alliance for Grieving Children (childrengrieve.org)

Support Services and Helplines:
1. National Suicide Prevention Lifeline (suicidepreventionlifeline.org)
2. Crisis Text Line (crisistextline.org)
3. SAMHSA's National Helpline (samhsa.gov/find-help/national-helpline)
4. The Trevor Project (thetrevorproject.org)
5. Veterans Crisis Line (veteranscrisisline.net)
6. Childhelp National Child Abuse Hotline (childhelphotline.org)
7. RAINN (Rape, Abuse & Incest National Network) Hotline (rainn.org)
8. GriefNet (griefnet.org)
9. HealGrief (healgrief.org)
10. Local Mental Health Agencies

Online Counselling Services:
1. BetterHelp (betterhelp.com)
2. Talk space (talkspace.com)
3. 7 Cups (7cups.com)
4. Online-Therapy.com (online-therapy.com)

These recommended readings, websites, and support services offer valuable resources for individuals navigating the complexities of grief. By exploring these materials and accessing support networks, individuals can find the tools, guidance, and community needed to navigate their grief journey and find moments of healing and hope.

Dedication

Gratitude and Recognition

This book is dedicated to all those who have experienced loss and are navigating the journey of grief. Your strength, resilience, and courage are a testament to the enduring power of love and the human spirit.

Special thanks to:

- The countless individuals who have shared their stories of grief and healing, providing inspiration and hope for others.
- The support groups, counsellors, and mental health professionals who offer invaluable support and guidance to those experiencing loss.
- The authors, researchers, and advocates who have dedicated their work to understanding and supporting the grieving process.
- The family and friends who provide unwavering support, love, and compassion to those navigating the complexities of grief.

May this book serve as a source of comfort, guidance, and hope for all who read it. Through the shared experiences and insights of others, may you find the strength and resilience to navigate your grief journey and find moments of healing and renewal.

Copyright Information and Legal Disclaimer

Beyond Tears: Navigating the Journey of Grief

Author: Dr. Bhaskar Bora

Copyright Information:

Legal Disclaimer:

The information provided in this book is for general informational purposes only and is not intended as, nor should it be considered a substitute for, professional medical advice, diagnosis, or treatment. Always seek the advice of your physician or other qualified health provider with any questions you may have regarding a medical condition or mental health issue.

The author has made every effort to ensure the accuracy and completeness of the information contained in this book; however, the author assumes no responsibility for errors, omissions, or for any consequences resulting from the use of the information provided. The content of this book is based on personal experiences, research, and reflections and is not intended to serve as professional or clinical advice.

Readers should consult their own healthcare providers regarding any specific medical conditions or concerns. The author and publisher disclaim any liability or responsibility for any adverse effects, injuries, or damages resulting directly or indirectly from the use of the information contained in this book.

Acknowledgements:

The author wishes to acknowledge the support and contributions of the individuals and organizations who provided their insights, stories, and expertise in the creation of this book. Your generosity and courage in sharing your experiences have made this work possible.

For permissions requests, please contact:

Dr. Bhaskar Bora
bora.dr@gmail.com